Virtue Ethics
Meditations on the Pagan Wheel of the Year

REV. LAUREL HOLMSTROM-KEYES

GREEN MAGIC

Virtue Ethics © 2025 by Laurel Holmstrom-Keyes. All rights reserved. No part of this book may be used or reproduced in any form without written permission of the Author, except in the case of quotations in articles and reviews.

Green Magic
53 Brooks Road
Street
Somerset
BA16 0PP
England
www.greenmagicpublishing.com

Designed and typeset by Carrigboy, Wells, UK
www.carrigboy.co.uk

ISBN 978 1 915580 26 9

GREEN MAGIC

Table of Contents

Introduction 5

Winter Solstice or Yule – Reverence 15
   Questions for Reflection – Reverence 23
   Reverence Ritual for Yule 24

Imbolc or Candlemas – Power 27
   Question for Reflection – Power 34
   Owning your Power Ritual for Imbolc 35

Spring Equinox or Ostara – Strength 39
   Questions for Reflection – Strength 45
   Strength of Character Ritual for Ostara 46

Beltane or May Eve – Beauty 49
   Questions for Reflection – Beauty 54
   Self-Blessing Ritual for Beltane 55

Summer Solstice or Litha – Mirth 57
   Questions for Reflection – Mirth 64
   A Mirthful Ritual for Litha 65

Lammas or Lughnasadh – Humility 68
   Questions for Reflection – Humility 75
   A Ritual to Cultivate Humility for Lughnasadh 76

Fall Equinox or Mabon – Compassion 79
   Questions for Reflection – Compassion 85
   Compassionate Forgiveness Ritual for Fall
      Equinox 86

Samhain or Halloween – Honor 90
   Questions for Reflection – Honor 97
   Honor your Ancestors at Samhain. 98

Afterthoughts 100

Introduction

There are many books that discuss the Wheel of the Year for Pagans. The names of the holidays, their meanings and mythology, their correspondences, and even recipes for each are easily found in books and online. Most Pagan holidays during the year have mythological stories associated with them or specific gods or goddesses that are linked to the holiday. Some see the Wheel of the Year in terms of the human life cycle. Some view the Pagan holidays as observing the changes in nature throughout the year. The discussions in this book are centered on a general understanding of the Wheel of the Year; however, I believe any Pagan tradition could adopt the approach of using virtue ethics to deepen our understanding of the ritual year.

Religion is a powerful force in human cultures. It tells us why we are here, how to live a 'good' life, ritualizes the human development process, tells us how to suffer, and helps us understand death and the afterlife. This series of meditations is focused on how to live a 'good' life from a Pagan perspective and to be a 'good person'. Virtues, in the pre-Christian understanding, could more properly be called 'Areteology', meaning an account (logos) of what is excellent (arete) in human affairs. This account describes not only the things someone does, but also the kind of person she is … to a virtuous person of the ancient world, the right questions were: what kind of person should I be? What kind of life should I live? What is an excellent human being like? What must I do to be happy? The general answer to questions like these went like this: "You have to produce within yourself a set of habits and dispositions, something like a 'second nature', which would give you full command over your powers and potentials. In other words, you have to transform your character."[1] This book is a discussion about what an excellent human being might be within a modern Pagan/non-Pagan context.

Another reason for a new look at our Wheel of the Year is related to religious symbols. Anthropologist Clifford Geertz[2] proposed a definition of religion which, in simple terms, describes the power of symbols to act on our moods and motivations, which then heavily informs our worldview, and if those symbols are used in ritual, then that worldview becomes what we see as reality, as 'really real'. We must be introspective about the symbols we create in a religious context as they are powerful in explaining reality in an, often, subconscious way.

Since I am a part of the LGBT+ community, I have often struggled with the traditional mythos and symbolism of the Pagan Wheel of the Year, which is primarily heterosexual in its presentation as well as heteronormative. Carol Christ, in her important essay titled *Why Women Need the Goddess*[3] describes the anguish she felt trying to find herself in traditional understandings of the (male) Christian God and Jesus. She argued that women have to deny their own

---

1 Myers, Ph.D., Brendan. The Other Side of Virtue: Where our Virtues Come from, what they Really Mean, and where they Might be Taking us. O Books, Winchester, UK, 2008.
2 Geertz, Clifford. Religion as a Cultural System. From: The Interpretation of Cultures: Selected Essays. pp.87-125. Fontana Press, 1993.
3 Christ, Carol, P. Why Women Need the Goddess: Phenomenological, Psychological and Political Reflections. From: Spretnak, Charlene, Ed. The Politics of Women's Spirituality. Anchor Books, Garden City, New Jersey, 1982.

personhood to see that they belong to that understanding of the divine. Queer folk have also had to do mental gymnastics with traditional Pagan understandings derived from Gerald Gardner and the beginnings of Paganism, which were heterosexually based. I thought about a lesbian Wheel of the Year, but did not find that prompted a deeper understanding of Paganism; nor did seeing the holidays as observing the natural world provoke a deeper thea/ological understanding. This is not to deny the power of nature or the beauty of the changing seasons. Something inside myself wanted more. As I studied at Cherry Hill Seminary to become a Pagan Community Minister, I thought about how we could develop deeper Thea/ologically as Pagans and was prompted by the work of Brendan Meyers to think about a virtues-based framework for our religious year.

I have always loved *The Charge of the Goddess* by Doreen Valiente[4] and find this section of her liturgy particularly useful for this discussion: "Let my worship be within the heart that rejoiceth, for behold: all acts of love and pleasure are my rituals. *Let there be beauty and strength, power and compassion, honor and humility, mirth and reverence within you.*" While Valiente saw the Pagan Rede – do what you will, and it harm none – to be the ethics of witchcraft, I find her listing of virtues to be of spiritual import and an ethical basis for Pagans, as I will argue in this book.

---

[4] The Charge of the Goddess. [Starhawk contends in The Spiral Dance that this is traditional and no one knows who wrote it. Others argue that Doreen Valiente wrote it. The version used in this book is based on the version in The Spiral Dance.] Starhawk. The Spiral Dance: A Rebirth of the Ancient Religion of the Great Goddess. Harper & Row Publishers, San Francisco, 1979.

THE VALUE OF VIRTUES

Virtue ethics is a philosophy inspired by Aristotle. Aristotle was a Pagan living in Greece within a polytheistic culture. His philosophical ideas came from observations of the natural world and his own logical reasoning. He argued that being a good person meant cultivating virtuous character traits over time. For our purposes here, we do not need to go into detail about Aristotle's philosophy. Rather, cultivating virtuous character traits over time fits well with the Pagan notion of the Wheel of the Year and visiting various themes at each point of the wheel throughout our lives.

"Virtues afford a stable psychological position for contemplation and guidance. They are a psychological mindset that provide a behavioral compass, offering the framework and driving force for living a life whose mission statement is practical self-improvement and social enhancement".[5]

Using virtues in our ritual year promotes reflection on our own personal growth in practical ways, no matter who we are. It starts to articulate what being a 'good person' is for our Pagan traditions. It is important for us to understand what being a 'good person' is in our traditions. This is a typical topic for many religions. I believe this is an important conversation for Pagans to engage in and discuss. To have virtues we agree on and aspire to develop in ourselves could help us be more civil to each other in our disputes within Paganism. While I have not been part of nor participated in such disputes, I have heard about them and read about them. While differences of opinion are to

---

5 (https://www.psychologytoday.com/us/blog/envy-this/202212/why-virtue-matters-today).

be expected, how we debate and discuss those differences is another matter. By claiming and articulating what being a 'good person' is in Paganism, we have a basis of virtues to help any disagreements or disputes that we may have, to draw from the same set of principles to help us find equitable solutions. Indeed, defining a 'good person' in Paganism would help in every aspect of our lives.

The notion of a good person is not meant to be a value judgement. Because one person is good according to this list of virtues does not mean that someone who does not aspire to these virtues is bad. We are only articulating what a person may aspire to within our spiritual understanding. Certainly, other religions have precepts or guidance on what a good Jew means or a good Christian or a good Muslim or a good Hindu. For Pagans, we would clearly see this effort as a process and not a goal. Since Pagans typically see newborn humans as already good; this virtues approach would help us *maintain our goodness* throughout our lives. The Oxford Dictionary defines goodness as "the quality of being morally good or virtuous." Pagans have not discussed what is moral or virtuous very often due, I believe, to the influence of the Pagan Rede or the association of this discussion with strict dogmatic morality found in Abrahamic religions. However, the ancients were concerned with morals and virtues before the Abrahamic religions began, so this discussion is firmly within our Pagan past – as evidenced by the previous discussion above regarding Areteology. Pagan philosophers of today may wish to articulate these ideas in more depth, which would be very welcome.

I noticed that the eight virtues in *The Charge of the Goddess* map onto our Wheel of the Year, and I have matched them as: Reverence – Winter Solstice/Yule; Power – Imbolc; Strength – Spring Equinox; Beauty – Beltane; Mirth – Summer Solstice; Humility – Lughnasadh; Compassion – Fall Equinox; Honor – Samhain. This framework for the Wheel of the Year is inclusive. Anyone can be beautiful, strong, powerful, compassionate, honorable, humble, mirthful and reverential. Perhaps other Pagan traditions might see different virtues for these or other holidays, or maybe some would put these virtues at different points of the Wheel, and that is great. The idea here is to contemplate the virtues associated with each point on the wheel and how we are evidencing such virtues in our own lives, whatever symbolic framework we use. Anyone, of any gender, sexual orientation or any other category of identity can work with these concepts without denying any part of their identity. As a white, cisgendered woman, I may not always see my privilege in this writing, and for that I do apologize in advance. I offer this sincerely as a perspective that can be changed to embody any set of virtues that appeal or are culturally relevant. I do hope this might engage a discussion in the Pagan world and that we might find a common set of virtues or, at least, understand each other's.

As we move around the year, we may be confronted with many different issues during our lives which would prompt a somewhat different approach to any of these virtues. For example, how we might demonstrate compassion or humility may show up in a variety of ways throughout our life. One year compassion might be shown to marginalized people, another year it may be shown to a family member or towards one's self. This framework for our Wheel of the Year is not meant to be a measurement or another way to judge each other. Rather, it is an invitation to meditate on these virtues and see how they speak to us, and if embodying these virtues improves our lives and relationships.

As I see the Wheel of the Year, the Solstices and Equinoxes are celestial events. They mark events we can see, even if incrementally. The cross-quarter days – Imbolc, Beltane, Lughnasadh and Samhain call us to the mysteries, the imaginal and the liminal. I use the Celtic names for the cross-quarter days as they are familiar to me and many Pagans. Feel free to use whatever names you give them. There are suggestions for rituals in this book. I presuppose you have a Pagan practice already. If you are new to Paganism, I recommend *The Elements of Ritual* by Deborah Lipp, *The Spiral Dance* by Starhawk or *The Grimoire of the Green Witch* by Ann Moura as good starting points.

The prayers are meant to promote further contemplation and enhance personal practice. A definition of prayer that would appeal to Pagans is found on Wikipedia: "Prayer is an invocation or act that seeks to activate a rapport with an object of worship through deliberate communication. In the narrow sense, the term refers to an act of supplication or intercession directed towards a deity or a deified ancestor. More generally, prayer can also have the purpose of thanksgiving or praise, and in comparative religion is closely associated with more abstract forms of meditation and with charms or spells."[6] We have a rich tradition of Pagan prayers, reaching back 4,000 years. I highly recommend *A Year of Pagan Prayer* by Barbara Nolan[7] to learn about this amazing resource of spiritual inspiration.

---

6 https://en.wikipedia.org/wiki/prayer [While I don't often use this source for definitions, I found this entry useful.]

7 Nolan, Barbara. A Year of Pagan Prayer: A Sourcebook of Poems, Hymns and Invocations from Four Thousand Years of Pagan History. Llewellyn Publications, Woodbury, MN, 2021.

Prayer is a very personal practice. Even though some religious faiths pray together, Pagans have only a few short prayer-type liturgies that most are familiar with. When I taught Feminist Theology at a university, one year I did a section on prayer and discovered that the topic of prayer was definitely more personal than the topic of sex to my students. Formal prayers are often poetry or types of speech that are different from everyday life. Improvised prayers may be spoken in everyday language. In whatever form we pray, we are seeking rapport with our deities or ancestors or the natural world for reasons personal to us. Try the prayers included in this book as an open door to the virtues through another avenue. Perhaps families may try the prayers together.

As we think of a wheel as symbolizing our ritual year, we can also focus our attention on what is in the center of the wheel. I propose that love is at the center, the *unconditional love* that is the center of ourselves, the life force energy that flows through all living things. As a professional clairvoyant, I have seen and personally witnessed such unconditional love as the core of who we are. Such an understanding flows naturally with the Pagan understanding that we are born 'good'. Everyone has access to this unconditional love, but not all people know this. The further a person is from their core of unconditional love, the less loving, kind, and understanding of others they are. The personality which is created when we enter the body at birth may obscure our unconditional love for a variety of reasons. Returning to the understanding that the core of ourselves is unconditional love and that we only need to move out of the way for that to flood our consciousness is another goal of this approach to our Wheel of the Year. As we work with these virtues, we have the ability to see them paired with love, which brings us closer and closer to the unconditional love we all possess. As we align with the changing tides of the seasons in our rituals, we are participating in the flow of life, the mystical energy of this amazing planet, which draws us closer to the primal life force of unconditional love.

In this discussion, I will be drawing on the theory of Biocentrism.[8] Biocentrism is a scientific theory that proposes that many of the conundrums of physics can be reconciled by placing *consciousness* into all equations. Biocentrism draws on quantum theory, many-worlds theory and classical physics. It argues that our experience of the world is created in our *minds*, that we are the observers in the universe that make it come into existence. Space and time are logical constructs of the mind only. They do not exist physically 'out there'. Even color cannot be found in the physics of light, it is our minds that perceive red or blue. The ability we have for memory creates the impression of time, and time is seen as how our minds perceive change in the universe. While I do not understand biocentrism mathematically, I do see it as re-framing our notions about how the world works and find it fascinating to ponder in a Pagan and magikal context. Notice here that I have not used the word 'brain'. The brain is the organ through which consciousness is experienced, much as light and sight are experienced through our eyes. We will explore how biocentrism relates to Pagan understandings to some extent in this examination of virtues.

A book is linear by its very design. The Wheel of the Year is a circle, a spiral, and thus cannot be truly captured in a

---

[8] Lanza, M.D. Robert; Pavsic, Matej and Berman, Bob. The Grand Biocentric Design: How Life Creates Reality. Ben Bella Books, Dallas, TX, 2020.

linear design. Therefore, this book can be opened at any holiday you choose and can 'start' at any point on the wheel. I chose Yule to 'begin' the book and Samhain for the 'end'. Basically, this follows the understanding of Yule as birth and Samhain as death. I see those both as liminal times and thus full of possibilities and potentials. A good way to begin this journey.

As we travel the wheel and focus on each virtue for that point on the wheel, we can move more toward becoming excellent human beings. The rituals and prayers at the end of each section are meant to help you engage with the virtues and help you consider them more specifically in your own life. *The Charge of the Goddess* asks us to be powerful, strong, beautiful, mirthful, humble, compassionate, honorable and reverent with love at the center of all.

Power (and love) – Imbolc or Candlemas – February 1.
Strength (and love) – Spring Equinox or Ostara – March 20–22.
Beauty (and love) – Beltane or May Eve – May 1.
Mirth (and love) – Summer Solstice or Litha – June 20–22.
Humility (and love) – Lammas or Lughnasadh – August 1.
Compassion (and love) – Fall Equinox or Mabon – September 20–22.
Honor (and love) – Samhain or Halloween – October 31.
Reverence (and love) – Winter Solstice or Yule – December 20–22.

Winter Solstice or Yule – Reverence

After our meditations on death at Samhain, we turn our attention now to re-birth and the growing of life after death's rest. At Winter Solstice, the darkness begins to lift and the days begin to become lighter longer. Many cultures mark this time by using light, usually in the form of candles, to symbolize this change in the seasons.

Reverence is defined as deep respect for someone or something and derives from Old French and from the Latin reverentia, from revereri 'stand in awe of.' The definition of awe includes wonderment as well as fear and dread. Unpacking this aspect of awe, we can see the influence of Abrahamic religion's notions of deity as we see fear in this definition. Certainly, we can understand why some fear the unknown or the incomprehensible. However, Pagans reject such notions and ask why should we fear the gods/goddesses, fear the unknown? We seek relationship with our deities, not to be cowered by fear. Reverence with love, wonderment with love, allows us to experience the magnificence of life itself in all its glory. This could be our encounters with deity or our experiences of nature on this planet that are truly awesome – the Grand Canyon in the US, the Iguazu Falls in South America, the majesty of the Swiss Alps, the abundant colors of fall or the fish of the coral reefs, the Earth itself from space, the Waitomo Caves in New

Zealand, and so many other incredible examples on this planet of life's amazing ability to make us wonderstruck.

Being reverent takes us out of ourselves. We are focused on our object of reverence or awe. We are bathed in the utter surrender to the magnificence of what we revere. To be able to give oneself over to that sense of wonderment can take us back to our childhood, where all was new and small things brought us wonder. If our childhood was difficult, this process can help us reclaim that sense of wonder as adults. Or perhaps as we grew into our adult selves, we stopped feeling reverence and awe in small things, stopped being curious or inquisitive. At Yule, we can allow ourselves to find that again. We see here in this virtue that a good person, being Pagan, can feel awe and reverence for life, that this ability can create joy in our lives, can humble us before the awesomeness of our incredible home, Earth.

Let's stop here though, and contemplate what having reverence in the dark might signify. Being Pagan, we do not see the darkness as negative. Darkness is the rich, mysterious place where we encounter deity, where seeds start their journey, where the stars reside, where the growing baby lives in the womb until birth. Darkness takes us deep inside ourselves to discover the wondrous self that is us. In darkness, we dream. In meditation, we 'see' in the darkness, allowing us to commune with deity, uncover and engage our own shadow for healing and find the calm space within for renewal. We can 'stand in awe' of the darkness, of all that it provides to us.

Seeds are a perfect symbol for this time of year. Part of the cycle of plant life and animal life, the seed is the continuation of life renewing itself. The seed's path is to grow; much as the path of our own lives in our current bodies is to grow and change as we age. Are we giving ourselves good watering, good nourishment, enough light to grow towards? And clean air to allow ourselves to breath in and out easily? Are we stuck in a pot that is too tight for our roots or are we allowing ourselves to reach and grow easily? Do we need support at times to grow towards our light? Do we embrace life in all its magnificence – including joy and sorrow?

We can also direct our minds to re-learn that darkness is to be revered, not feared, as a step in our anti-racist journey. The US culture, among others, has too long regulated darkness as indicative of evil or wrongdoing, which is symbolically and literally harmful to people of color. Symbols are powerful and must be used with awareness. How different we all might feel to see darkness with reverence, to see darkness as rich with possibilities, fertile soil for growing a magnificent life. Pagans have an opportunity here to teach others that darkness is not to be feared, that the unknown is the unmet and we draw strength by opening our arms and establishing relationships with the 'unknown' so that we can see clearly and without bias.

Some see birth as a potent symbol for the Winter Solstice, as the Sun returns and begins to grow towards fullness at Summer Solstice. We may use the symbolism of the mystery of the goddess giving birth to the god, who will grow and change as she does, as she becomes the Maiden at Imbolc. Depending on where we live in the Northern Hemisphere, we may not actually see the Sun on the Winter Solstice, but we know it is there and have certainty that the hours of light will gradually grow longer as each day passes. Some cultures believed that the rituals performed at the Winter

Solstice actually helped the seasons to continue. At Winter Solstice, we can reverence life itself, the animating force of the universe that flows through all things. When we feel anxious or unsure, we can reflect on this certainty. Nature shows us that the seasons follow one another in constant rhythm. We do not need to believe. We can see the natural world and how it changes. The regular procession of the seasons gives us something to hold on to, even in the midst of uncertainty.

Scientist Robert Lanza, in his groundbreaking book *Biocentrism*[1], offers this profound statement: "Life creates the universe, instead of the other way around." Life is not a by-product of this world, but the actual force that creates it. We can definitely stand in awe of this perspective. It forces us to re-think our notions of life itself and recognize that life does not necessarily begin at birth. Rather, life *creates us* on an ongoing basis. How awesome is that?!

Actual human birth is also awe-inspiring, to which most people who have witnessed a birth will agree. I have had the experience of witnessing both birth moments and death moments, each a truly amazing experience. It makes sense that we would feel reverence at the returning of the light, and the experience of birth, whether an actual human birth or the birth of a creative activity, or the birth of a new identity.

Richard Sima, writing in *The Washington Post* in 2022[2], shows that the experience of awe is "associated with living healthier and more meaningful lives. A 2021 study reported that feeling more awe is correlated with reporting feeling lowered levels of daily stress. Intriguingly,

---

1 Ibid.
2 https://www.washingtonpost.com/wellness/2022/09/15/awe-mental-health/

people who feel more awe also tend to have lower levels of inflammatory cytokines. Positive experiences of awe have also been found to increase feelings of well-being, life satisfaction and sense of meaning." Thus, the cultivation of awe and reverence in our lives is good for our physical and mental health as well.

At this time of year, there are so many traditions to draw upon to enhance our reverence. A solstice tree in our home, a Yule log patiently waiting, a hearty feast, giving and receiving, and music to lift our hearts on the longest night of the year. We may have cultural traditions from our families for this time of year. See if you can find the reverence in those. Perhaps it is the reverence of ancestor traditions, perhaps it is that walk in the woods or the beach. How do you feel when awestruck? How does bringing oneself into a state of reverence enrich your character? What is awe-inspiring in your life this year? What moves you to wonderment? Consciously, allow such experiences into your life. Seek them out. Your answers to these questions can offer clues to where you may need to engage with the virtue of reverence more deeply. We may find that being reverent also engages our humility, which is another spoke on our Wheel of the Year. Many of these virtues are linked to each other.

When we consider reverence and love, we can see that reverence is a form of love, or that awe can bring love forward in us as we experience awe itself. We may see an amazing sunset and feel the love of that experience fill us with wonder. One aspect of awe is that we never want it to end. If a sunset filled us with joy, we are eager to experience one again. Our experiences of awe bring forward love that is unconditional, which mirrors the core of who we are and thus brings us closer to our true beingness. How awesome we would be to radiate unconditional love to all we meet.

Many of our Yule traditions bring us together with our loved ones. We can practice reverence for our elders, for the newborns. We can consciously look for the awe in our loved ones' smiles and laughs. By continuing family or chosen family traditions, we are revering our ancestors. Perhaps we can set a place at the table for them, if they have left the body. Perhaps we can welcome a stranger to our table to give them an experience of awe. There are so many ways to find reverence and awe at this time of the year.

We can see the incredible lights people put up on houses for 'Christmas' as a reminder of awe and reverence. Many light displays cause us to stare with smiles on our faces as all the lights are reflected in our eyes. We may not be able to take ourselves away and feel sad to have to leave. The Northern Lights in the far north sky can offer another chance to feel awe. Even our own Yule or Christmas trees can bring awe into our homes when only the tree is lit and all the other lights are turned off.

The Star card in the tarot shows us that the experience of reverence and awe may bring us to a peacefulness within ourselves. We can approach wholeness, openness and healing at this time of year. Awe and reverence bring us into present time so we can perceive divine energies moving from death to birth, or rest and action. In our families, we can open ourselves to more love or to the beginning of love. We can start anew, if we desire; or integrate all the growth we've had since Samhain or throughout the last solar year. The magical energy of healing in the quiet of a snowfall or a warm fire or wonderful feast brings the Star to life.

This is a great time to recite *The Charge of the Goddess* in rituals or at your altar. The Star Goddess is our own Sun, which is a star, whose light grows anew with the New Year, and the Charge helps us be reverent of her. I offer it here in two versions – one with the goddess speaking, and one as the worshipper speaking:

The Charge of the Goddess Regarding the Star Goddess – Reclaiming Version[3]

Hear the words of the Star Goddess, the dust of Whose feet are the hosts of Heaven, whose body encircles the universe:
I Who am the beauty of the green earth and the white moon among the stars and the mysteries of the waters,
I call upon your soul to arise and come unto me.
For I am the soul of nature that gives life to the universe.
From Me all things proceed and unto Me they must return.
Let My worship be in the heart that rejoices, for behold, all acts of love and pleasure are My rituals.
Let there be beauty and strength, power and compassion, honor and humility, mirth and reverence within you.
And you who seek to know Me, know that the seeking and yearning will avail you not, unless you know the Mystery: for if that which you seek, you find not within yourself, you will never find it without.
For behold, I have been with you from the beginning, and I am That which is attained at the end of desire.

To the Star Goddess:

> *You who are the beauty of the green earth*
> *And the white moon among the stars*
> *And the mysteries of the waters,*

---
[3] https://reclaimingcollective.wordpress.com/charge-of-the-goddess/

You call upon my soul to arise and come unto you.
For you are the soul of nature that gives life to the universe.
From you all things proceed and unto you they must return.

Your worship is in the heart that rejoices, for behold-
All acts of love and pleasure are Your rituals.
Let there be beauty and strength, power and compassion,
Honor and humility, mirth and reverence within me.

And as I seek to know you, I know that my
Seeking and yearning will avail me not, unless
I know the Mystery:
For if that which I seek, I find not within myself,
I will never find it without.

For behold, you have been with me from the beginning,
And you are that which is attained at the end of desire.

Use the questions at the end of each holiday with your family, yourself, coven or spiritual friends to delve deeper into the virtues for yourself.

WINTER SOLSTICE OR YULE – REVERENCE

QUESTIONS FOR REFLECTION – REVERENCE

Does the poem above help you to see reverence or invoke reverence for you? Why or why not?	
What experience has evoked the most awe in your experience?	
Why do you think that experience gave you a sense of awe or reverence?	
How do you see darkness?	
What Solstice traditions help bring reverence or awe into your life?	
What about the experience of reverence helps you become a good person?	

REVERENCE RITUAL FOR YULE

For this ritual, you will need one small votive candle, either white or green, and one white taper candle on your altar. Prepare incense of your choice. If you have a tarot deck, put the Star card on your altar for the season or put an image of the Sun. You may want to record the meditation, so you can listen and visualize. If you use cakes and ale in your rituals, prepare those beforehand.

Prepare yourself by dressing in ritual clothes and washing your hands.

Ground yourself as you typically do.

State your intention: *I come before the powers of the universe in reverence to awaken my spirit with awe.*

Light your small votive candle and incense. Let the rest of the room be dark.

Set up your circle in your typical format. I suggest casting the circle three times – once with your athame, once with blessed water, and once with incense. Call the quarters as you typically do.

If you have specific goddesses or gods you wish to invoke, do so now. Make an offering to them as appropriate, or say *The Charge of the Goddess*.

Stand in the center of your circle. Bring yourself into the moment and approach stillness. Visualize the stars above you, the Sun which is our own star that shines its power onto the Earth, the stars who gave you the ingredients for your body and bring the energy of the stars into your body.

WINTER SOLSTICE OR YULE – REVERENCE

Visualize the ocean and rivers of the Earth, the waterfalls, the ponds, and the tides, the blood that flows through your veins. Bring the energy of the Earth's waters into your body.

Visualize volcanoes erupting, the heat of the desert, the humid air of the equator, the reptiles that bask in the sunshine, the passions of your life. Bring the energy of volcanoes into your body.

Visualize the vast mountains of the Earth, the backbones of the planet, the majestic peaks with snow, the sure-footed animals that walk the mountain paths, the bones in your body. Bring the energy of the Earth's mountains into your body.

Take a deep breath.

Visualize the Moon shining her light across the waters, across the valleys, across cities and towns. She shines for all. Her light shines in your heart. Bring the energy of the Moon into your body.

You are now filled with the powers of the universe. Take a moment to feel those powers within you. The stars swirl around you as the waters return to the sky, the mountains receive the water back as snow and the volcanoes warm the planet for growth, while the Moon in its fullness covers the land in her magical light. Feel gratitude for the awesome connections between all the powers of the universe and your place within those connections. Bask in the feeling of reverence for all of life and the awesomeness of love in your life.

Take a deep breath.

At your altar, hold the votive candle in your hand and, using the powers brought within you, bade farewell to the end of the solar year with your own words.

Light the taper candle and snuff out the votive candle.

Welcome the new solar year with any words that you typically use or that come to you spontaneously.

If you use cakes and ale in your rituals, offer them first to the goddesses or gods you invoked and then enjoy what you prepared with them. As you eat and drink, think about your experience and if you feel more reverent. If so, how? If not, why not?

When you are finished with the cakes and ale, thank the goddesses and gods for sharing time with you. Bade them farewell.

Release the quarters.

Open the circle.

You may offer a benediction: *Blessings have been given; blessings have been received. May the awesome energy of the goddess/god/universe be ever in my heart. The ritual is ended.*

Touch the ground/floor.

Perhaps after the ritual, you could watch an awesome movie or look at awesome pictures you own or online. Take a walk in the snow or the rain or the heat.

Imbolc or Candlemas – Power

We move now from honoring the darkness at Samhain and revering life itself at Winter Solstice to considering the virtue of power at Imbolc. The Gaelic word Imbolc identifies the time of initiation and the activity of initiation itself. When we initiate, we are powerful, we are beginning something, coming into a new state of being. At this point in the Northern Hemisphere, we are just starting to visibly see the days grow longer, watching for the last frost date so we can begin our veggie gardens. We may be actually being initiated into a Pagan tradition or self-initiating as a solitary practitioner, or we may be initiating something we thought of between Winter Solstice and now. Whenever we step into a new role or a new plan of action, we can consider power.

Our dictionaries need to update their definitions of power. Power is defined as "the ability to control people and events."[1] This is only one definition of power. In Starhawk's discussion of power[2], she makes a distinction between *power-over* (the current definition) and *power-with*. Pagans are in an excellent position to demonstrate power-with. In initiation, we are demonstrating power-with. The purpose

---
1 https://www.merriam-webster.com/dictionary/power
2 Starhawk. Truth or Dare: Encounters with Power, Authority and Mystery. Harper & Row, New York, NY, 1987.

of initiation in our traditions is to welcome a person into a tradition to learn, to grow and to become the best they can be in that tradition. The initiator is not evidencing power over the initiate, even if they completely dominate the initiation ritual. Rather, they are providing a powerful spiritual experience for the initiate to start them on their journey. When we share power with others, our wisdom increases – we can become more than we are individually. Together, we can create spiritual groups or helpful organizations or social justice movements.

There is another aspect of power to consider from a Pagan perspective – the power we raise when we create magick. Most magical workers understand that some type of power is needed to boost our visualizations and intentions magically and, at times, send our magical workings to a specific person or place or thing. Different traditions see this power in different ways, but what *is* the power we wield in our magical workings? A new approach to this question can take biocentrism into account. Biocentrism states that "what we perceive as reality is a process that involves our consciousness. An external reality, if it existed, would by definition have to exist in the framework of space and time. But space and time are not independent realities but rather tools of the human and animal mind."[9] Thus, our consciousness is a key aspect of the power of our magic to manifest our desires. Starhawk describes magic as "the ability to change consciousness at will."[10] In magical workings, we change our consciousness to see what we desire as *having already happened*. This shifts the focus of our consciousness to enact a process that allows what we desire to come into being. This is a natural process, according to biocentrism, and one that only requires the power of our focus and intention. A power that is self-referent and self-directed towards our own well-being.

Personal power, located in our third chakra, is the ability to stand up for ourselves when needed and the ability to be our true selves completely, knowing our strengths and challenges. Meditations on personal power are excellent at this time of year. Children, in particular, would benefit from understanding power-with and personal power from a young age. To counter gender norms in our culture, girls can be encouraged to develop their ability to stand up for themselves, and boys can be encouraged to understand that power-with is more important than power-over. Non-binary children can benefit from both conversations. Families can demonstrate power-with among family members to develop healthy ideas about power among all family members.

Meditating on personal power, we must also consider our privileges. Some of us may hold only one or two privileges and others may hold many. A few hold none in our culture. By privilege, I mean those ways we are given the benefit of the doubt because of the way we were born – it bestows us with a certain amount of power in our society. Since I am white, I have white privilege. But as a lesbian, I do not have heterosexual privilege. Once we understand where our privileges lie, we can start to consider how to use such privilege to help those without such privilege. This is using power wisely. When we are given the power of privilege, it is up to us to wield it virtuously. Coming from the perspective of power-with, we can start to shift our understandings to see all the Earth's children as worthy of power-with and respect. Listening is an excellent way to begin. For men, this may be listening to women; for white women, this may be listening to women of color; for cisgendered people, it may be listening to trans or other gendered people; for people living in the US, it may be listening to our Native People. Listening carefully, without thought as to what we will say or what we think. Listening to hear is an important skill to consider for personal development. Try it out and experience the power of listening.

Listening can also help us understand the other 'persons' that surround us, such as other animals, plants, minerals and rocks and places of power where we live. We may also have relationships with non-physical beings, where power dynamics must be negotiated and honored. This animist perspective helps us take power out of human-only interactions and apply it to all our relationships with the physical and non-physical worlds.

At Imbolc, we can also consider our physical power use. As Pagans, we want to live sustainably on our Mother Earth and now is a good to time to assess your power consumption. Can you conserve more energy in your home? Are you turning off all lights when a room is empty of humans? Is it time to purchase a more energy-efficient vehicle or appliance? Are you ready and able to put solar panels on your home? Can you advocate for wiser energy use in your community? No matter your financial situation, there are things you can do to help our environment by assessing your everyday power use and finding ways to live easier on the planet. What a great time to initiate a plan for wise energy use. This is a plan the whole family can participate in and is an excellent demonstration to children of Pagan values.

Now, let's consider the *power of love* and the *love of power*. First, the love of power is seen in all the autocrats or dictators in history, as well as autocratic bosses or even parents. Love of power is not real power from the perspective of Pagan virtues. All leaders need to guard against this, since power is gained in leadership. Love of power eclipses most other emotions and, to me, indicates a lack of self-understanding and self-confidence. Autocrats or dictators typically need constant adulation or unhealthy loyalty. The love of power can corrupt, and the seeking of ever more power eclipses all other endeavors.

In contrast, the power of love is seen in mother animals guarding their young, in incredible feats of healing, in helping someone in despair turn their life around or in very long-term, loving and committed relationships. The power of love can shift someone from being a member of the KKK to opening their heart to all people. The power of love is invoked in our circles when we say that we enter in perfect love and perfect trust. The power of love brings home the lost dog or cat. The power of love lifts us up to become the best people we can be. Love is at the center of our Wheel of the Year because unconditional love is the core of all beings, whether we know it or not. As Ann Moura states: "Love is the law and Love is the bond."[3] How does the power of love show up in your life?

Of the Major Arcana in the tarot, the Emperor symbolism gives us more ideas about power. One understanding of the Emperor card is a just society. Certainly, using power-with in our associations and organizations leads us to continue creating a just society. A just society gives all of us the freedom to pursue our passions and personal development. *The Light Seer's Tarot* sees the Emperor energy as "exercising

---

[3] Moura, Ann. Grimoire for the Green Witch: A Complete Book of Shadows. Llewellyn Publications, St. Paul, MN, 2003.

sovereignty over your own reality." A concept of power for meditation.

The Goddess Brigid is strongly associated with this time in our year. Her attributes (traditionally healing, poetry and smithcraft) illustrate power as healing, as the power of words and the power to shape our environment. She is a daughter of the Tuatha De Danaan, the magical peoples of Ireland who are sometimes seen as the fae or the source of faery stories. The power of Brigid is shown clearly in her continued worship as Saint Bridget. The power of love of this goddess could not be destroyed. Certainly, the power to heal has been revered throughout time. Poetry or other forms of creative language have held special magical significance since the time of the ancient Greeks and possibly earlier. At times, poetry can express our feelings and desire more powerfully than prose. The use of rhyme in our prayers and spells is common in Pagan practice. The power to shape our environment is a special *responsibility* of the human species. While other animals and even plant communities can re-shape the environment, humans have excelled in this beyond any other species. This is the reason why we must consider our power usage in our lives now and why we must strongly participate in any activity that can move us towards more sustainable living.

I offer this prayer for use at your altar or outdoors, with a fire safely burning:

> *Goddess Brigid, she who knows the power of speech, manifesting and healing, we implore you to let our inner power be known. Help us use our power wisely and for the greater good. Let your example permeate the world, so that power is creative and inspiring toward the good.*

IMBOLC OR CANDLEMAS – POWER

Help us to see the power of love manifest in all our relationships with all beings, visible and invisible. Let us use power gently upon the glorious Earth and help us come into right relationship with her energy. Let our creativity flow in all ways and let our words inspire others. Let our healing begin. Let us manifest our heart's desires through love and power all around. Blessed Brigid, hear our prayer.

QUESTION FOR REFLECTION – POWER

Think about times when you've had power and when you haven't had power. List them.	
Do you need to forgive yourself for any time you abused your power or used power-over?	
How does the power of love guide your life?	
Is your personal power strong?	
Can you stand up when you need to?	
If you are a leader, how do you manage power as you lead?	
How can you assess your power usage in your home, work, life? Can you become more sustainable?	
How does your personal power help you be a good person?	

OWNING YOUR POWER RITUAL FOR IMBOLC

To prepare, write a poem or a short story or just a paragraph about Imbolc or Brigid; and craft something physical – paint, knit, crochet, sew, build, craft with paper. Make a Brigid cross or have something that you've already made; and have a healing item you use or have made for another – crystals, herbs, spells, etc. Arrange one white candle, an image of Brigid, an offering plate or bowl, offerings for Brigid (milk, water, candles, blackberries, bread, ivy, coins, herbal teas, heather, spears). If you use cakes and ale, have them ready at your altar.

Set up your altar as you typically do, with your one candle for Brigid and her image with the offering plate in front. Have your writing, craft and healing item(s) at your altar.

Dress in clothes that help you feel powerful. Wash your hands.

Ground and bring yourself to stillness.

State your intention: *I come before the Goddess Brigid to strengthen my personal power with the wisdom of Brigid.* Light the candle for Brigid, and incense of your choice.

Cast your circle.

Call the quarters, emphasizing the power of each direction. Air – the power to shape and lift; Fire – the power to destroy and transform; Water – the power of empathy and love; Earth – the power to stand strong and protect.

Invoke Brigid.

You can use this invocation or, even better, write your own:

> *Goddess Brigid, beloved daughter of Danu.*
> *Bright one, Powerful one, Lady of the Sacred Flame,*
> *Come to me this night, your night.*
> *I come into thy presence,*
> *Goddess of the hearthfire.*
> *I come into thy presence,*
> *Goddess of the threshold.*
> *I come into thy presence,*
> *Goddess of brightness.*
> *I come into thy presence,*
> *Brigid of grace.*
> *Hail and welcome.*

Place your offerings on the offering plate.

Say: *Brigid, please accept these offerings which I bring for your pleasure.*

Be still for a moment to sense Brigid's presence.

Take your writing in your hand. Feel pride in your work. Whether you like what you wrote or not, feel pride in your effort. Read it out loud.

Say: *Goddess Brigid, bless the power of my words, let your power flow into these words. Blessed Be.*

IMBOLC OR CANDLEMAS – POWER

Take up the craft that you have at your altar. Marvel at your ability to create. Know that your creativity flows from the creativity that birthed the universe. Think about that for a moment.

Say: *Goddess Brigid, bless my power of creativity. Let your power flow into my creative experiences. Blessed Be.*

Take up your healing item(s). Think of all the healing you have given, even a smile to a stranger or kind word to a child. Think of the healing the Earth gives us freely, in her herbs, foods, waters and soil.

Say: *Goddess Brigid, your healing power lives in these (name what you have). Let your healing power flow into (this or these items). Blessed Be.*

Put your hands crossed over your stomach area, your third chakra. See the pulsing yellow color of this chakra.

Say: *I affirm my personal power is found in my words, my creativity and my healing. My personal power is strong and life-affirming (and say any other words that come to you).*

If you use cakes and ale, offer the first to Brigid. As you eat, consider how you use your power now and in the past. How do you want to use your power in the future?

Fill your body with gratitude for Brigid and use your own words to bid her farewell.

Release the quarters and close the circle.

Offer a benediction: *Blessings have been given; Blessings have been received. May the wisdom of the Goddess Brigid remain in my heart. So Mote It Be.*

Touch the ground/floor.

Spring Equinox or Ostara – Strength

At this time on our journey around the wheel, we come to the Spring Equinox. Some call this holiday Ostara. Equinox means balance and we see that night and day are equal in length at this time. We take a big breath now to ponder moving from the darkness of winter at Yule to the full light of the Summer Solstice. It's time to make sure our soil is ready for planting and, in many areas, the first seeds can go in the ground. At this breath moment, we balance ourselves to be in alignment with the season. To achieve balance, here at the Spring Equinox, we think about strength and how strength is needed for balance and what the virtue of strength means in a Pagan context.

Consider balancing exercises such as Yoga, the balance beam in gymnastics, Tai Chi practice, and dance. As we age, physical balance becomes more necessary to lessen the fear of falling. Establishing physical balancing practices in our youth can help us move into our elder years with confidence. Physical balancing practices require strength or help us gain strength. Strength of the physical body helps us in our everyday lives and helps the body maintain health. The Equinox asks us to bring some kind of physical balancing into our lives, or validate what we already do, or add to what we already do. Strength helps us lift that wood, that shovel, that box of books, walk that new dog, and many other things in daily life. Being strong is helpful to all people, no matter their gender identity or physical conditions.

The strength of life itself is astonishing. We see this so clearly at this time of year in the Northern Hemisphere when seeds start to sprout and push up from being in the darkness of the fertile soil. We may need to prune some of our plants or aspects of our life, so that new things may grow and flourish. Consider the plants that push up through the concrete in the cities, the persistence of nature to renew itself after a wildfire, a flood, a tornado or a hurricane. This demonstrates to us the strength of life, always seeking growth. As Pagans, we seek to understand what nature shows us. We too are seeking growth in our lives as human beings in this lifetime. I prefer this concept rather than that life has 'lessons'. To me, the lessons perspective signifies that someone else has created or determined what we need to learn. This is not my experience as a clairvoyant. Growth is on-going and within each growth period there are opportunities for new understandings or new ways of being. Yes, we may learn things, but what we grow into is unique to each person and guided by their own being-ness, that part of us that exists between and through all lifetimes.

Strength is also a matter of character. Strength of character can include trustworthiness, respect, responsibility, fairness, caring, and citizenship. Being worthy of trust is a requirement for most relationships with others and also for ourselves. Do we trust ourselves to do the right thing, no matter what? Respect for all beings in the physical world and the non-physical world is essential for living in a diverse world. All beings of the Earth deserve our respect, as they are our relations. If we are responsible

SPRING EQUINOX OR OSTARA – STRENGTH

and fair, others will respect us. Caring for ourselves, our loved ones, strangers we meet, our communities and the Earth herself is sure to help us be a good person. Living in a society, our participation in voting or serving in our communities helps us demonstrate our citizenship.

To put it another way, the strength of our character can be displayed each day. Are we trustworthy? Do we respect everyone, regardless of how they differ from ourselves? Are we responsible in all our activities? Do we fairly consider all points of view and the feelings of others? How do we show that we care for ourselves and others? What kind of citizens are we? Do we vote? Do we participate in our communities? What do you think contributes to strength of character?

As we are considering strength at the Equinox, we are not thinking about strength as a means of overpowering another or forcing another to do what we want. Strength as a virtue can only point to strength of character or the strength to be balanced. Being Pagan means that there is no need for overpowering another or forcing others in any way. Abuse of strength is shameful and does not display strength of character.

Two cards in the Major Arcana of the tarot are helpful in this discussion. There is the Strength card, which in many decks typically features a woman and a lion. The other card is the Hanged Man, which typically shows a man hanging upside down. *The Light Seer's Tarot*[1] states for Strength: "Step into patience and fierce serenity as you exert your graceful influence for the greater good." For the Hanged Man it states: "Open your heart to the bigger plan and you'll inadvertently tap in to a whole new framework from

---

[1] Chris-Anne. The Light Seer's Tarot Guidebook. Hay House, Carlsbad, CA, 2019.

which to see the world." Fierce serenity requires strength of character and a balanced perspective. The fierceness of our convictions bathed in the serenity of knowing our own truth, which does not negate others, brings new meaning to the idea of strength as a virtue. Knowing when we need a new point of view and taking the action to gain it requires strength. We may need to let go of something previously thought. We may be shocked by what we see, and turned upside down in our new awareness. We can see this profoundly in anti-racism work. No matter where we are in our awareness of the horrific realities of racism, we can always gain another perspective for ourselves. Reading *How to Be an Anti-Racist*[2], I was struck how Mr. Kendi described racist attitudes in himself. This reminded me of homophobia within the LGBT+ community. The strength we need to change ourselves to become anti-racist or rid ourselves of internalized homophobia goes far beyond any benefits of physical strength. The strength of our character is built in such a way that it cannot be lost.

We can now see that strength of character is found in relationships. How we interact with ourselves, our loved ones, our colleagues, even with those we disagree with helps us see our strength of character and give us insight into aspects of our character that may need more focused attention. If you find attributes you wish to have as part of your character, use your magical tools to develop such attributes, asking the elementals or your deities for assistance. Try the survey on this website to learn of your character strengths: https://www.viacharacter.org/. This will help you see where you are now and what you may need to work on.

---

2   Kendi, Ibram, X. How to be an Anti-Racist. One World, New York, NY, 2019.

SPRING EQUINOX OR OSTARA – STRENGTH

Strength with love brings to mind the way parents love their children, a person who accepts responsibility for their actions, and the grace we give another who may have hurt our feelings. The strength of our love can do so many wondrous things. We can turn that kind of love on ourselves and love ourselves fiercely, even with all our idiosyncrasies and challenges. The strength of our love can heal or renew a relationship or lift up another or turn us into activists for a noble cause. What has the strength of your love done in your life? Is this an area where you need more balance or more attention? The strength of your love might be a beautiful meal you cook for loved ones, the dance you do to bring a smile to a child's face, the song you sing for an elder in the nursing home, the prayer you share with a grieving person, or the sheer delight you find in your lover's eyes.

For Spring Equinox and the virtue of strength, we can look to two demigods of the ancient Greek world for prayerful inspiration. Atalanta, whose father desired a son, was raised by a she-bear, a symbol of Artemis. She was known for winning footraces against men. Aphrodite, who wanted Atalanta to dedicate to her, gave Hippomenes golden apples to win a footrace with Atalanta. He had fallen in love with her at first sight. The apples worked and various versions of the story describe how the couple turned into lions after sexual bliss.

Heracles, demonstrated extraordinary strength, courage, and ingenuity in his labors. While some required actual strength, others required intelligence and persuasion, as well as persistence and patience. He was seen as a hero and a god. Our modern idea of a hero derives from the ancient Pagan world.

Heracles, strong-armed son of Zeus and Alcmene
of the dark eyes, great one whose deeds are well-known,
whose ancient stories are yet told throughout the world,
whose glorious name will never be forgotten,
I praise and honor you. Lend me the wisdom of your labors
That I may also embody bravery and persistence in my own life.

Atalanta, favored of Artemis, you whose strength, speed and prowess were heralded throughout the ancient world.
You who excelled against the social norms of your sex.
I praise you and honor you. Let my own life be one of independence with the power of love leading me to transformations of my character.

QUESTIONS FOR REFLECTION – STRENGTH

Reflect on your strength of character. Take the survey on https://www.viacharacter.org/. Which character strengths do you already have and which can you intentionally enhance?	
What are the ethics that you would practice, even when no one is watching?	
Reflect on the strength of your body. How does it feel? What small thing can you do to increase your strength or flexibility?	
What do you love fiercely? How do you express that?	
What strengths of your character do you see that move you towards being a good person?	

STRENGTH OF CHARACTER RITUAL FOR OSTARA

To prepare, talk to a friend or family member about the questions in the ritual. Make notes and bring those to your altar. If you have a tarot deck, put the Strength card and the Hanged Man on your altar. Prepare one white taper candle in the center of your altar. Put six small candles in a semi-circle around the taper. If you use cakes and ale in your rituals, prepare them beforehand.

Dress in ritual clothes. Wash your hands.

Ground yourself, deeply and strongly.

Light the incense of your choice.

State your intention: *I call upon the strong ones of the ancient world, to help me see the strength of my character.*

Cast your circle as you did at Yule, three times with athame, blessed water and incense.

Call the quarters, focusing on the strength of each element. Air's strength to inspire us. Fire's strength to ignite our passions. Water's strength to transform our lives. Earth's strength to persist.

Call on deities that you see as embodying strength of character, or call upon Heracles and Atalanta.

SPRING EQUINOX OR OSTARA – STRENGTH

Light the taper, saying: *My strength is sacred. I come before the divine to dedicate my strength to sacred purpose.*

Hold the first small candle on the left of your taper in your hands. Say: *This is how I am trustworthy.* Speak what family or friends say about your trustworthiness. Now speak your own words for becoming more trustworthy in your life. Light the candle with the taper. Say: *My trustworthiness is a sacred aspect of my strength of character.*

Take the next small candle in your hand. Say: *This is how I am respectful.* Speak what family or friends say about your respectfulness. Now speak your own words for becoming more respectful in your life. Light the candle with the taper. Say: *My respectfulness is a sacred aspect of my strength of character.*

Take the next small candle in your hands. Say: *This is how I am responsible.* Speak what family or friends say about how you are responsible. Now speak your own words for becoming more responsible in your life. Light the candle with the taper. Say: *My ability to be responsible is a sacred aspect of my strength of character.*

Take the next small candle in your hands. Say: *This is how I am fair.* Speak what family or friends say about your fairness. Now speak your own words for becoming fairer in your life. Light the candle with the taper. Say: *My fairness is a sacred aspect of my strength of character.*

Take the next small candle in your hands. Say: *This is how I am caring.* Speak what family or friends say about your caring. Now speak your own words for becoming more caring in your life. Light the candle with the taper. Say: *My caring is a sacred aspect of my strength of character.*

Take the next small candle in your hands. Say: *This is how I am a good citizen.* Speak what family or friends say about your citizenship. Now speak your own words for becoming a better citizen in your life. Light the candle with the taper. Say: *My citizenship is a sacred aspect of my strength of character.*

Take a moment to breathe and allow the words you have spoken to go deep within your being. Say: *Here at the Spring Equinox, when I seek balance in myself, my strength of character balances my life.*

If you use cakes and ale, offer the first to any deities that you invoked, or to Heracles and Atalanta.

When finished, thank the deities or Heracles and Atalanta for sharing the time with you and bade them farewell.

Release the quarters.

Open the circle.

Offer a benediction: *Blessings have been given; Blessings have been received. May the strength of Heroes and Heras remain in my heart. So Mote It Be.*

Touch the floor or ground.

Beltane or May Eve – Beauty

After reviewing our strength of character, we arrive at Beltane, one of the liminal holidays that encourages us to consider beauty as a virtue. It may seem odd that beauty can be a virtue until we consider all the ways the word beauty can be used. In the dictionary, the word beauty is defined as "the quality present in a thing or person that gives intense pleasure or deep satisfaction to the mind, whether arising from sensory manifestations (as shape, color or sound), a meaningful design or pattern, or something else (such as a personality in which high spiritual qualities are manifest)." Now, we can see more clearly how beauty works in our Pagan calendar. A personality in which high spiritual qualities are manifest. We might even consider that embodying all the virtues in this framework of our Wheel of the Year can show us what a beautiful personality would look like.

Beauty is not only found in nature and its abundance of beautiful things, such as a sunset or sunrise, the Grand Canyon or the Himalayas. I've heard mathematicians say that when a mathematical equation is right, it looks beautiful. We say beauty is in the eye of the beholder to signify that what is beautiful to one may not be beautiful to another. The definition above points to that, since what is seen as a meaningful design or pattern would change between people. Additionally, what gives each of us intense pleasure or deep satisfaction may be quite varied. What we consider beautiful in another shows us who we are attracted to for sex, for companionship, for friendship or for marriage or other deeply committed relationships. What we find beautiful may help us decide how to decorate our home, our bodies, our altars or our surroundings.

Typically, at Beltane Pagans will celebrate sexuality and dance around the Maypole, which are clearly suited to contemplating beauty at this time. As stated previously, who we find beautiful or attractive is different for each person. As Pagans, we want to celebrate any kind of attraction as long as it follows our Rede – do what you will, and it harm none. Thus, Pagans would never advocate for any sexual activity that actually disrespects another. Rather, we want to celebrate sexual expression in all its forms as a natural part of human existence and a pathway to ecstasy. Ecstatic states bring us into the spiritual realm, where we can profoundly feel our interconnectedness with all things while being grounded in the body. In ritual, we dance and chant to bring us to ecstatic states, and dancing around the Maypole gives us a glimpse into such realms.

We also make ourselves beautiful to attract mates or please ourselves. I must admit, as a Libran, I do appreciate when others try to look their best, and I try to look my best as well. This pleases me because beauty is satisfying to me. As we consider what beauty means to us personally, it is also a good idea to consider what cultural messages have been received about beauty. How a woman or a man or a non-binary person is supposed to be beautiful versus how someone feels beautiful in themselves is a good way to begin. Standards of beauty do not serve us and condition us to believe that certain characteristics are beautiful, and we rarely ask ourselves if that is true for us. We need to see all types of bodies, colors, and other characteristics as beautiful, while still being cognizant of what we are personally attracted to. Cultural ideas are powerful though, and it takes consistent work to uncover our own information. Many LGBT+ people grew up seeing and hearing that opposite sex people should be attracted to each other and that your body determines your gender. It takes courage and relentless self-examination to come to the understanding that one is attracted to the same sex or that one is not cisgendered.

We can appreciate those who create art of any kind, from paintings to photography, and books to movies, fashion designers and illustrators. The ability for an artist to capture meaning with or without words is a wonder. Their efforts can take us away from our everyday lives or give us insight into our own lives. We can dream of possibilities and learn about human experiences we may never have. Art does not always have to be beautiful; the creative act is what is beautiful, no matter what the art looks like. Whether beauty is intrinsic or created, we can revel in it under the maypole.

We can have beautiful personalities. Psychology tells us that empathy, positivity, authenticity, humility (another virtue on the wheel), kindness, resilience, and integrity make up a beautiful personality. Empathy, the ability to put yourself into another's shoes and truly understand another's feelings, helps us connect deeply to others. We cannot be positive all the time, but positivity helps us light up a room with our presence. Being true to oneself, our authenticity, we find in the ancient world, as *know thyself*. These are a crystallization of our journey around the wheel each year. Even in the mythos of the wheel, we learn more about ourselves. Humility we will visit at Lughnasadh. The kindness we express can help us be happier and more satisfied with our lives. Resilience is more and more needed in our times, given climate change. The more we can bounce back from setbacks, the healthier we will be. Being honest, standing up for yourself and keeping your word, integrity, is one of the most beautiful aspects of a personality. A person with integrity is trustworthy.

We can embody beauty by loving ourselves no matter what. Often, we may find that we are critical of ourselves, for various reasons, and our spiritual goal is to always return to loving ourselves. Thus, beauty and love have an intimate relationship. Why is it important to love ourselves? Actually, it is more about uncovering the love that is the core of our being. We are already filled with unconditional love as life force flows through us, but our personalities and experiences often make it difficult to remember that truth. Getting out of our own way is a good metaphor for the goal of uncovering our own internal sense of unconditional love for ourselves and others. Consider the life force flowing through all things. In nature, there is no judgment – life just flows, creates, transforms and seeks balance. The more we learn about nature's processes, the more we see how interconnected we all are on so many levels. We can see nature as the embodiment of the life force flowing freely through all things, and isn't that beautiful?

When we can feel the love that is the *core of our being*, we are more ready to enter a relationship in a healthy manner. This holds true for all relationships, whether romantic or not. A quick search online about beautiful personalities lists other qualities, such as being modest, embracing our flaws, being able to laugh at ourselves, being good listeners, being kind, and leaving a positive impression. It could be a fascinating family or coven discussion to see what others think is a beautiful personality.

Many Pagans create beautiful altars for worship and to bring in the energy of the season. Many Pagan rituals are beautiful, with candles burning in the dark, flowers, gourds, and stones. Many of us enjoy dressing up in ritual clothes of various styles to help us feel more magical and to feel beautiful. Thus, our Pagan spirituality enjoys beautiful images which may or may not appear beautiful to those outside our circles. While outward beauty is pleasing, inward beauty is even more wonderful. What do you think makes for a beautiful personality? How would that relate to being a good person as a Pagan?

The Lovers card in the tarot can be a guide for this turn of the wheel. While it typically indicates a relationship, is it also about choices. *The Light Seer's Tarot* challenges us to "fall into trust in order to create lasting bonds … Remember that self-love is the key to balancing the duality of any relationship."

QUESTIONS FOR REFLECTION – BEAUTY

What do you find attractive?	
What do you see as beautiful?	
Describe your understanding of a beautiful personality?	
How can your understanding of beauty contribute to your understanding of a good person?	

SELF-BLESSING RITUAL FOR BELTANE

During Beltane, a self-blessing is a great way to ritualize loving ourselves and bring ourselves into relationship with our ideas of deity as it relates to our body. I have seen a few versions of the self-blessing and first encountered it via Z. Budapest.[1]

If you can be naked during this, all the better. Otherwise, dress in clothes that help you feel beautiful. A self-blessing is also lovely to do with a sexual or romantic partner, where you each bless each other.

Decide what you will use to anoint yourself. Water or a wine/water mix is typical. Decide which deity you want to address or if you want change the language to fit your purpose or perspective.

Stand and ground. Have your anointing liquid ready.

Declare: *Bless me Mother (or deity of your choice), for I am your child.*

Anoint your eyes saying: *Bless my eyes to see your ways.*

Anoint your nose saying: *Bless my nose to smell your essence.*

Anoint your lips saying: *Bless my lips to speak your name.*

Anoint your breasts saying: *Bless my breasts, formed in strength and beauty.*

---
[1] Budapest, Z. Self-Blessing Ritual. From: Christ, Carol, P. and Plaskow, Judith. Womenspirit Rising: A Feminist Reader in Religion. Harper & Row Publishers, San Francisco, CA, 1979, p269.

Anoint your genitals saying: *Bless my genitals that bring me pleasure and could bring forth life as you have brought forth the universe.*

Anoint your feet saying: *Bless my feet to walk in your path.*

Take a moment to notice how it feels to bless your body. Do any more words come to you?

Please feel free to adapt this to your personal circumstances, bodies and ideas. I believe a self-created self-blessing would be all the more powerful. A self-blessing is an affirmation of life, of loving oneself no matter what and connecting to the Divine. Talk about beauty with your family, lover(s), children and coven mates.

Summer Solstice or Litha – Mirth

Why wouldn't we put mirth at the Summer Solstice? We have been awed by reverence, owned our power, strengthened our character, and considered the beauty of our personality. It's time to take a break and laugh. Mirth is defined as: "Amusement, especially as expressed in laughter and also being merry." Merry is defined as: "Cheerful and lively and characterized by festivity and rejoicing; slightly and good-humoredly drunk." When Pagans say 'Merry Meet' and 'Merry Part', we are saying that we meet in cheerfulness and we depart in cheerfulness. While some rituals are somber and serious, the Summer Solstice is time to 'lighten up'. This is an apt characterization since the Sun's 'light' is the longest of the year.

Mirth reminds us not to take ourselves too seriously. We are reminded that laughter is also sacred. Think of the story of Amaterasu, the powerful Asian goddess, who was tempted out of her cave by a bawdy dance that made her laugh and brought the 'Sun' out into the world again. Think of the sacred clowns who "deflate the ego of power by reminding those in power of their own fallibility, while also reminding those who are not in power that power has the potential to corrupt if not balanced with other forces, namely with humor."[1] Notice here how the virtues around

---

1 https://fractalenlightenment.com/25726/spirituality/the-path-of-the-sacred-clown-where-trickster-and-shaman-converge#:~:text=The%20

the wheel influence each other. If we can balance our power with humor, we are much less likely to become corrupted by that power.

Laughter is also good for our health. The short-term effects of a good laugh enhances our intake of oxygen-rich air, stimulates our heart, lungs and muscles, and increases the endorphins that are released by our brain. Laughter can relieve our stress response and decrease our heart rate and blood pressure. Laughter stimulates circulation and aids muscle relaxation. Over the long term, laughter can boost our immune systems, relieve pain and help us feel good about our lives. Think of the times you have had a good laugh and how good that felt or maybe you remarked, "I needed that."

The laughter and merriment of children lifts our hearts and reminds us to visit our child selves and play again. Acting out stories or myths in ritual can be very fun and provoke laughter in a ritual setting while retaining the power of the myth. At the Summer Solstice, with its emphasis on fire rituals, we can remember sitting around the fire, telling stories, laughing as our s'mores dripped on our hands or back into the fire. If we have the ability to jump a bonfire at Summer Solstice, we can ask that our cares and troubles be lifted so that we can feel our joy and mirth. We can make a solar wheel to carry our woes and watch them burn away in the fire. Certainly, laughing at our fears or troubles is an excellent way to lessen their power on us and make room for positive changes.

Returning to the role of sacred clowns, we also want to be mindful of not laughing at others' misfortunes or

---

main%20function%20of%20a,other%20forces%2C%20namely%20with%20humor situations. If they are laughing, we can laugh with them, but we cannot find mirth in the misfortune of others. This goes against the virtues of compassion and humility, also found on our Wheel of the Year. Paganism is made up of all sorts of people, and the Discordians are a great bunch to get you laughing – they would probably laugh at my attempt to ascribe virtues to the Pagan holidays. The Learn Religions website tells us that "Discordianism was founded in the late 1950s with the publication of the *Principia Discordia*.[2] It hails Eris, the Greek Goddess of Discord, as the central mythological figure. Discordians are often also known as Erisians. The religion stresses the value of randomness, chaos, and disagreement. Among other things, the first rule of Discordianism is that there are no rules." Learn Religions continues: "Many consider Discordianism to be a parody religion (one that mocks the beliefs of others). After all, two fellows calling themselves Malaclypse the Younger and Omar Khayyam Ravenhurst authored the *Principia Discordia* after being inspired – so they claim – by hallucinations in a bowling alley.

Discordians can argue that the act of labeling Discordianism a parody merely reinforces the message of Discordianism. Just because something is untrue and absurd does not make it without meaning. Also, even if a religion is humorous and its scriptures full of ludicrousness, it does not mean its followers are not serious about it." Thus, even modern Paganism has its sacred clowns, who tell us to laugh, throw away the rules and be silly and spiritual at the same time.

---

[2] Beyer, Catherine. An Introduction to Discordianism. Learn Religions, Oct. 29, 2020. learnreligions.com/discordianism-95677

I was drawn to Paganism because it was fun, among other reasons. It was a radical idea for me at the time, but I thought why shouldn't religion be fun? Who said religion had to be serious and somber all the time? Engaging in our practices as Pagans has great meaning, but many of them are also fun to do. Crafting our tools, our altar cloths, our spells can give us a sense of enjoyment and pleasure, as well as meaning. Dressing up in our witchy garb takes us out of ordinary reality and prepares us for magic and mystery and the joy of feeling *ourselves* as magical and mystical. Singing together in a circle is fun. Holding hands and dancing together is fun. Jumping the bonfire is fun. While all these activities have deeper meanings, the pleasurable aspect of them is worth recognizing. Indeed, we can reflect back on *The Charge of the Goddess*: "All acts of love and pleasure are my rituals." When we laugh, when we feel pleasure in our lives, we are close to the Divine.

During my one and only LSD experience, I was sitting on a cliff at the beach. I could feel the energy of the Sun and the waves flowing through me as if I was the one making the waves move. As I did this, I found myself laughing at the thrill of this experience and felt absolutely connected to all the natural forces and forms around me. While I am not suggesting this technique to everyone, psychoactive substances have been part of religious worship in many cultures. When I was studying Californian Native American culture in college, I learned that the Chumash in Southern California regularly used psychoactive substances to make their art. Research on psychoactive substances is promising to help people with depression and addictions in microdoses. Certainly, some strains of marijuana and hashish bring on much laughter. While we must be very careful using such substances and be mindful of those whose addictions do not allow such experiments, within our traditions there is room for exploration for those inclined and properly guided.

As a family or a coven, you might tell jokes this day, or watch a funny movie, watch a stand-up performance or anything else that provokes laughter after any ritual for the holiday. Even your ritual could be humorous. Ticklefests can be fun with children, but first make sure that they like it. Talk about the difference between humor that puts people down and humor that lifts people up, or is just plain funny without hurting anyone. Play a game or give witty toasts. Dance and twirl until you get dizzy on purpose. Find out what kind of humor everyone has or what they find funny. Do they like slapstick, irony, satire, dark humor, witty wordplay, topical humor? Who are their favorite comedians? Our pets can bring us great joy and laughter just being themselves. I always chuckled when my beagle mix would paw at her blankets to get them just right on her bed.

Mirth and love are easy with each other. How often have you heard one person in a couple explain that they love the other because "(they) make me laugh." Just as in other aspects of our lives, gentle humor in a relationship is a pleasure and a shared laugh is a wonderful and intimate experience. The more we 'lighten up' about ourselves, our issues, and concerns the closer we can get to that feeling of unconditional love we all crave. In my psychic training, we had to look at many of our own issues in the beginning of the training, and the teachers would always say when we were looking at difficult things to 'be amused'. This meant to bring our energy to the level of amusement in order to look at hard things from a different perspective. As with the Hanged Man in the tarot, sometimes we need to change the view, and humor can be the wave we can ride to a new understanding. The Queen of Wands in the tarot brings her fiery nature into our circles and *The Light Seer's Tarot* tells us, "make sure fiery bursts are accompanied by laughter and gratitude."

At Summer Solstice, let's invite Eris to our rituals and allow laughter to run free. Let's become drunk on our own joy and merriment, if not our own wine, if we desire. Changing our consciousness through trance, or meditation or psychoactive substances is all part of the human story where we take a peek into the realms of spirit, which teaches us that the 'unseen' world sits right next to us … and laughs with us.

A Hellenic Invocation to Eris:

> *Homage to thee, O Eris, at thy beautiful chaos. Of all that is Sweet, of all that is Bitter, thou hast domination over all. Hail Eris! Hail Discordia! O divine madness, self-created, self-anointed, self-serve, thou art Goddess of Heaven and Earth, thou did create beings celestial and terrestrial. Live thou in me, and I in thee, O thou Golden Apple of the Sun!*[3]

Discordian Meal Prayer:

> Eris Good and Strong and Bright,
> Make this food safe tonight.
> *Anthrax, chicken pox and hugs,*
> *Please keep at bay such thugs.*

---

[3] https://vocal.media/futurism/ways-of-worship-eris

Kitty claws and dragon teeth,
Do not contaminate my beef.*
My veggies and salads green,
Are not replaced with dolphin spleen.

Eris, O Mother Discordia and poof,
Take this as prayer, not spoof.
Through your guidance and strife,
May we see our lessons in life![4]

*Vegetarians may change this to:

Kitty claws and dragon sneeze,
Do not contaminate my cheese.

---

4 https://www.adf.org/pt-br/articles/gods-and-spirits/hellenic/eris.html

QUESTIONS FOR REFLECTION – MIRTH

What funny movies, books or jokes can you use at the Summer Solstice to bring on mirth?	
How would you include laughter if jumping the fire at midsummer?	
What would you use in circle, with family or with yourself to 'lighten up' Summer Solstice?	
Reflect on how laughter feels in the body. What do you notice?	
Consider how not taking oneself too seriously can move you towards being a good person.	

A MIRTHFUL RITUAL FOR LITHA

To prepare, have a few jokes, riddles or funny limericks memorized or written down. This ritual is best with a Pagan family or group of Pagans. Prepare a cauldron with charcoal and an herb you have around the house whose scent you enjoy, and be ready to light it. Prepare fun food for cakes and ale.

Dress in colorful clothes or whimsical clothes. Wash or sanitize your hands.

Ground.

State intention: *We gather on this Summer Solstice (morn, eve, day) to bring laughter to the world, to lighten up our energy before the turning of the wheel on the longest day of the year.*

Cast the circle with everyone skipping around the circle, singing: *The circle is cast, we are having a blast!*

Call the quarters, inviting each to bring their mirth to the circle – for Air to bring inspired wit, for Fire to bring bawdy humor, for Water to bring puns, and for Earth to bring slapstick humor. For more fun, give an example once you have called the quarter.

Call on any deities you see as mirthful, or call on Eris, Goddess of Chaos, to join in the rite.

Prepare the cauldron and charcoal. Light the charcoal and when it is ready, add the herb you've chosen. Place the cauldron in the center of the circle and ask each person to step over it, stating what they desire to release to experience more joy. Once each person steps over the charcoal, they can act out the releasing. Laughter is appropriate at any time during this ritual.

Once all issues have been released, sit together in the circle and tell jokes or read your limericks. Each person gives their offering. See how the laughter is filling the circle. Encourage Eris to show herself. When the joke-telling is completed, do the Hokey Pokey (if you do not know how to do that, look it up on YouTube). Have fun with this!

Once the Hokey Pokey is done, bring out your fun food and drink and offer the first to Eris or whomever you have called to join in. Tell funny stories or recall funny memories you have.

> When finished eating, hold hands in the circle and sing:
> *Air Moves Us, Fire Transforms Us.*
> *Water Shapes Us, Earth Heals Us.*
> *And The Balance Of The Wheel Goes Round And Round.*
> *And The Balance Of The Wheel Goes Round.*

This calms the energy so you can focus now on ending the ritual.

Release Eris or any deities that you have called with praise and thanks.

SUMMER SOLSTICE OR LITHA – MIRTH

Release the quarters, speaking how you enjoyed their mirthful gifts.

Open the circle, see all the mirthful energy gather together as everyone walks widdershins (counter-clockwise) in a spiral to end up in the middle of the circle as a tight group.

Breathe. Take in the energy of the ritual, the mirth and the releasing. Move back out into a large circle and touch the floor or ground.

Offer blessings to each other.

Lammas or Lughnasadh – Humility

At this point on the Wheel of the Year, we arrive at our first harvest. If you are a gardener, then you know that many vegetable plants are now coming to fruition and are ready for harvesting. Check in with your local environment. Learning what is coming to fruition at this time of year can help you plan your rituals as well as also helping you become more connected to the place where you reside. Doing all we can to grow food and still being dependent on weather brings to mind the virtue of humility or the ability to be humble. The definition I prefer for humility in a Pagan context is not being proud or arrogant, but being modest, being humble and successful.

Proud, in this context, refers to having or showing an inflated or excessively high opinion of oneself or one's importance. This sort of pride often goes with being arrogant and both show us that they are geared towards ourselves only. Prideful and arrogant people are difficult to get along with and can be destructive to a group trying to achieve a goal or a coven wanting to gel. This sort of pride should not be confused with the pride that comes from achieving something wanted or attempted, or the pride we feel in others and their achievements. Thomas Merton wrote: "Pride makes us artificial and humility makes us real."[1]

Being modest and humble may sound old fashioned; however, being modest means being unassuming and not giving excessive importance to what you are doing or achieving. Being humble keeps us grounded. Being humble helps us refrain from becoming arrogant. We learned about being powerful at Imbolc. Here, at Lughnasadh, we consider how to be powerful *and* humble. Our ability to develop the virtue of humility helps us to not become enamored of our power or our position in life or an organization.

"A humble person is more concerned about what is right than about being right, about acting on good ideas than having good ideas, about embracing new truths than defending outdated positions, about building the team than exalting the self, about recognizing contribution than being recognized for it."[2]

Traditional meanings of this time of the year for Pagans are centered around the act of dying, and sacrifice, so that the community may thrive. John Barleycorn, from English folklore, is the embodiment of this notion. He is one name of a deity of this time that sacrifices himself, so that his own body may be used for food and drink. To me, this demonstrates a profound level of humility. We do not even need to personify the grain or any plants to realize that they give us the greatest expression of being humble. They are just who they are, with no fanfare or pride. Spending time in nature and observing the plants and animals can help

---

1 https://www.brainyquote.com/quotes/thomas_merton_378759
2 Covey, Stephen, M. R. Trust and Inspire: How Truly Great Leaders Unleash Greatness in Others. Simon & Schuster, New York, NY, 2020.

us understand humility further. A tree or a squirrel does not need to boast about itself or tell anyone what they are doing, yet they are magnificent just existing.

One way to help ourselves be humble is to foster a sense of gratitude towards life and towards others. At this first harvest time, it makes sense to focus on gratitude, since we can easily be grateful for the bounty of the garden or the farmers' market. We can be grateful for any achievements we have made since Imbolc. We can be grateful for the coming dark time of the year, when we will go deep within ourselves to integrate the learning and experiences we have had since Imbolc. There is so much to be grateful for. In a state of gratitude, we are naturally humble.

A daily gratitude practice is well worth the time. It puts us in the frame of mind to be content with what we have or to be magically in a place of receiving what we desire. For example, many years ago I was living without running water or electricity. It was not a desired state of being. My partner and I were exposed to the gratitude practice developed by Louise Hay. So, each night, we were grateful for running water and electricity. Soon, the 'landlord' of the property we were living on gave us running water and electricity! This experience showed me an important aspect of magic. We must put ourselves in the energy of having received what we desire, so that it can manifest in our experience. Gratitude is a terrific way to bring us to that energy, and remaining in a state of gratitude leaves doubt out of the equation and prepares us to humbly accept what we desire.

The positive aspects of gratitude are astounding. Here is just one nugget from the web:

Neural mechanisms that are responsible for feelings of gratitude have grabbed attention.[3] Studies have demonstrated that at the brain level, moral judgments involving feelings of gratefulness are evoked in the right anterior temporal cortex.[4] People who express and feel gratitude have a higher volume of gray matter in the right inferior temporal gyrus.[5] And the Mindfulness Awareness Research Center of UCLA stated that gratitude changes the neural structures in the brain, and make us feel happier and more content.[6]

It is important to note that being humble does not mean being a doormat or being so self-effacing as to be demeaning to oneself. Being humble or having humility is a quiet, calm understanding of our worth that does not need to be shouted or compared with anyone else. While we may value humility as Pagans, our culture in the US does not particularly show the true meaning of humility. Our media is more apt to show people being arrogant or mean to each other than being humble and grateful. The rise of social media influencers does not promote humility as a virtue. Many of our politicians do not promote humility as a virtue.

---

3 Wood, A.M.; Maltby, J.; Stewart, N.; Linley, P.A. and Joseph, S. A Social-Cognitive Model of Trait and State Levels of Gratitude. Emotion Vol. 8, No. 2, 2008, pp281–290.

4 Zahn, R.; Moll, J.; Iyengar, V.; Huey, E.D.; Tierney, M.; Krueger, F. and Grafman, J. Social Conceptual Impairments in Frontotemporal Lobar Degeneration with Right Anterior Temporal Hypometabolism. Brain, Vol. 132, issue 3, 2009, pp604–616.

5 Zahn, R.; Garrido, G.; Moll, J. and Grafman, J. Individual Differences in Posterior Cortical Volume Correlate with Proneness to Pride and Gratitude. Social Cognitive and Affective Neuroscience, Vol. 9, issue 11, 2014, pp1676–1683.

6 https://newsroom.ucla.edu/stories/gratitude-249167

We may also know Pagan leaders that are not humble and appear more self-serving than community-serving.

It seems then that cultivating humility in our lives is a radical act. Being humble *and successful* is a model of a balanced human being. Being clear-minded about our achievements and successes and calmly and quietly affirming our pride to ourselves as well as giving credit where credit is due and not letting our heads swell with pride helps us demonstrate this virtue in our daily lives. Humility means we can feel pride in what we do, but we feel that pride within ourselves. We want to use that as self-affirming. Self-validation is the best way to be validated, since seeking it from others will never work out well. If others observe what we do and appreciate what we do, then we can take that in to enhance our own self-validation and quietly accept the compliment. However, self-validation, once cultivated, is always available whenever it is needed. "Validating ourselves is important because it is a way for us to accept and better understand ourselves. By receiving our feelings and thoughts, good or bad, we are giving ourselves grace and allowing ourselves to be our truest selves. Self-validation can then lead us to have a stronger identity and to better manage the range of emotions we feel."[7] Self-validation is beneficial to our mental health and a gratitude practice supports positive self-image.

Looking at humility in context with the other virtues under discussion, we can see how humility helps us to not take any of them to extremes (power, mirth, strength), and other virtues (compassion, power, reverence) help us to not take humility too far into self-invalidation. Since we use a wheel to describe our Pagan holidays, we can see that all

---

7 https://oregoncounseling.com/article/practicing-self-validation/

LAMMAS OR LUGHNASADH – HUMILITY

the spokes on a wheel must be equal in length, or else the wheel will not turn properly. All these virtues are equally important to cultivate in our character and they help us become balanced people with love at our core.

The Hermit tarot card encourages us to go within, to seek our inner guides and inner wisdom. Our inner life is where humility lives. Our deep knowing that we are worthy and have the inner guides to help us be successful is the challenge of the Hermit. *The Light Seer's Tarot* reminds us that "in the deepest trenches of self-discovery, we must remember that our continual search for our own healing and inner truth does not mean we are not already whole and healed."

Humility is love's repose. Love is not arrogant or proud. Unconditional love is peaceful and comfortable. It does not need to shout or prove itself to anyone else. It rests in the knowing that it is worthwhile intrinsically. When we are humble, we are demonstrating the peace of love. We are allowing our love to flow to others and resting in the clear knowing that our humility is increasing our understanding of love in action. We are feeling that we are intrinsically worthwhile and humbled by that understanding when it becomes part of our sense of self.

> "In our human life, when we have something, immediately pride, vanity and many other undivine forces enter into us. We extol ourselves to the skies. But let us think of the example of a tree. When the tree is in full bloom, when it is laden with ripe fruits, when it really has something to offer the world, the tree bows down. If we can become one with the consciousness of

a tree, we will feel that the more we have to offer, the more humility we will have."[8]

Oh Aidos, Goddess of Humility, the last to leave the mighty Earth after the Golden Age, sister of Nemesis, she who keeps us humble and respectful, smile upon me now. Let my heart know the peace of your gifts, so that I may walk in the world with understanding and love. She who helps us know our worth quietly, but deeply, bring me to a clear understanding of how humility improves my life. Let me find my self-worth through your presence in my life and by the good deeds I do when no one is watching. All praise, Aidos, Goddess of Humility, may humility be my guide.

---

[8] https://www.srichinmoylibrary.com/ca-2

QUESTIONS FOR REFLECTION – HUMILITY

What examples can you find of humble people in your life or in literature or films?	
What would humility look like in your family, your coven or among spiritual friends?	
What would humility and success look like in your life?	
Do you have a gratitude practice or can you start one?	
Do you give gratitude at meal times? Before bed? In the morning?	
Do you offer gratitude to your deities? How can they assist you in becoming more humble?	
How does humility contribute to being a good person?	

A RITUAL TO CULTIVATE HUMILITY FOR LUGHNASADH

To prepare, gather pictures of deciduous trees and plants that you love and place them on your altar. Have one green candle on your altar. Prepare simple food for your cakes and ale. If you drink alcohol, beer is particularly appropriate at this Sabbat.

Dress simply and wash your hands.

Ground.

State your intention: *Gratefully, here at this turning of the wheel, I come to learn about humility.*

Cast your circle, feeling pride in your ability to do so.

Call the quarters as you typically do.

Call on Aidos, Goddess of Humility, using your own words or the following:

> *Aidos, Goddess of Humility,*
> *The last to leave the mighty Earth after the Golden Age,*
> *Return now, riding on my gratitude for your gifts.*
> *The gift of humility,*
> *The gift of respect,*
> *The gift of modesty,*
> *The gift of inner guidance.*
> *Aidos, join with me today,*
> *As I seek your wisdom for my life.*

When you feel her presence, listen to her. Ask her what humble activity you might undertake in the next month. You might pick up trash in your town. You might find a volunteer opportunity. You might participate in a community garden or offer help with a harvest.

Once you have made your decision, dedicate yourself to the task in the presence of Aidos.

Now, look at the pictures of deciduous trees and plants. Use your imagination, a gift of the goddess, to consider how these plants and trees move through birth, death and rebirth, whether we see it or not. They move through their growth and death and re-growth with no fanfare or boasting. Flowers may put on quite a show, but they do not do that for praise. They are humble and successful. They are successful because *they are what they are*. Consider your own life. Do you live as you are? Or do you live to others' expectations? To society's expectations? Identify one way you can change how you live in the world to be more of who you are.

Prepare your cakes and ale for offering. First, offer to Aidos. Hold your food in your hands, and say: *As this is a gift from Aidos, I add my energy to this food to help me live as I am, humble and successful.*

Thank Aidos for her wisdom and bade her farewell.

Release the quarters.

Open your circle.

Offer a benediction: *Blessings have been given; Blessings have been received. May the humility of Aidos remain in my heart. So Mote It Be.*

Touch the floor or ground.

Fall Equinox or Mabon – Compassion

The Fall Equinox or Mabon is our second harvest holiday and some even call this the Witches' Thanksgiving. Equinoxes call us to seek balance in our lives. We stop here to regain our balance again since the Spring Equinox, and prepare for the underworld time of year. Days are becoming shorter, the air is getting crisper, and some of us will see the rain starting. We might find ourselves wanting a warm sweater at night or reveling in the last hot days until next summer. When we think of balance, we think of centering. That which is balanced is on its center, waiting there patiently, moving only slightly to maintain that balance. Did you start any balancing practices at the Spring Equinox? Now is a good time to check in on your progress. Have you become lax or lazy? Have you kept it up and deserve a pat on the back? Did you find that what you thought you would like, now seems to *not* bring you any joy? What new practices are you willing to try?

Many religions have borrowed from other faiths or have similar practices. Paganism in general has not often looked to Judaism for inspiration. However, I see that this time of year for Judaism has wisdom to offer us. In the Jewish tradition, the period between Rosh Hashanah and Yom Kippur is a time of asking for and giving forgiveness, of entering the New Year with a clear heart. As Pagans, we can also approach our New Year, Samhain, with a clear heart. How wonderful to approach our ancestors with a heart cleared to allow our love to shine forth. Maybe forgiveness is needed for a past hurt from a loved one who is no longer in the body. Maybe forgiveness is needed for something we've done that hurt another. How can we approach forgiveness as Pagans?

I see compassion as the route to balancing ourselves and finding forgiveness at this time of the year – compassion for ourselves as growing, living beings and compassion for others. Compassion derives from the Latin – compati – to suffer with. Here we find our Pagan answer to a theological question: *how* to suffer. Most religions entertain this question, with Buddhism seeing this as the most profound question of all. Pagans experience all kinds of suffering, as all people do in any other faith. Here, we can see that our ritual year holds a place to consider suffering and how compassion can help us – to suffer with. For Pagans, we would want to learn how to suffer with each other, to be compassionate, to be completely present with each other and to affirm that all our situations and experiences are valid and worthy of our compassionate presence.

Compassion brings empathy into action. Through empathy, we see and attempt to understand another's feelings. Compassion calls us to suffer with each other, to not only see the pain or hurt of others, but to actively engage in another's pain and hurt. This is a challenging practice. To allow the pain or hurt of another into our consciousness can open us up to our own pain and hurt. As we suffer with each other, we affirm the human condition of joy and pain. We affirm our species as caring, empathetic beings. We may even seek forgiveness in this sharing.

When we forgive, we shine compassion's loving attention onto hurts we have caused others, or those that have caused us hurt. For some of us, only by cultivating compassion can we even consider forgiveness. Forgiveness releases ourselves primarily. It does not excuse bad behavior. Rather, forgiveness can open us up to a compassionate understanding of what has harmed us. We may only be able to find compassion for another by seeing them as another hurt human being – not validating their choices, but recognizing that hurt human beings are not at their best. We can also choose not to forgive. If that is our path then compassion for ourselves is crucial. We are not wrong or unexamined or in denial if we do not see a way to forgive. And we need to give ourselves compassion for our own choices, knowing that we all are changing, growing beings walking our paths this lifetime.

Embodying compassion can help us with perspective-taking. This term denotes truly attempting to understand another point of view or another way of seeing the world. "Compassion is related to increased happiness and decreased depression. Self-compassion buffers the impact of stress via self-kindness and positive cognitive restructuring. Self-compassion buffers against anxiety, and is linked to increased psychological wellbeing. Compassion and empathy are fundamental aspects of quality relationships as they enable kind and loving behavior. Compassionate behavior such as volunteer work also has been associated with positive outcomes such as increased academic aspirations and self-esteem among adolescents (Kirkpatrick, Johnson, & Beebe, et al., 1998), as well as improved mortality rates among older volunteers (Yum & Lightfoot, 2005)."[1]

Compassion and love show us that we can also see that suffering with another demonstrates our profound connection to all other beings on this wondrous planet. "Earth, as well as all other living systems, has a magnetic field and scientists are discovering that these fields connect us all, and actually carry biologically relevant information. This information is suggesting that, not only can your actions affect yourself and others around you as well, but so can your thoughts, feelings and emotions. The way you feel changes the information coded into your magnetic field."[2]

When we are compassionate with love, we radiate that into our aura and our magnetic field, which in turn affects others near and far from us. Imagine all Pagans focusing on compassion with love at the Fall Equinox!

Take some time during the Fall Equinox to contemplate any relationships that require forgiveness. Look for ways to bring your compassion into action. Given that this Equinox is a harvest time, we might spend our time volunteering for a food bank or feeding the hungry and homeless at a shelter. In our homes, we can celebrate with luscious feasts that bring the foods coming to ripeness in our area to the fore. Over dinner, we can discuss forgiveness and compassion. Perhaps the family can create ritual together to find a safe space for airing hurts with patient listening and compassion, and seeking forgiveness or offering forgiveness in a sacred space. Those who are interested, and have the

---

[1] https://positivepsychology.com/why-is-compassion-important/#necessary
[2] https://www.collective-evolution.com/2018/11/29/scientists-explain- how-earths-magnetic-field-connects-all-living-systems/?fbclid=IwAR0Otn5 cdJZ-9XIrRo_BUIBYKRYtfnqolwsEq0H7kfJx7lF2dSdXSDbQSSQ

ability, may start to can fruit and veggies for the depths of winter, to care for the family in the coldness.

The Empress tarot card offers us another view of compassion, the kind of compassion that comes from a mother's unconditional love. The Empress is often equated with the Earth and nature – our guide to moving towards the unconditional love that is the core of each of us.

As we live our lives until Samhain, we can offer forgiveness and compassion to all we meet and endeavor to make all our relationships clear and loving – embodying *The Charge of the Goddess* in our journey around the wheel, offering compassion with love to our magnetic fields which will affect all our relationships.

KUAN YIN

Many of our pantheons in the Pagan past do not show us compassionate deities. However, we can look to the Asian pantheons for assistance. Kuan Yin is seen as the Goddess of Mercy and Compassion by many in Asia. It is said that she was a male god originally and then turned into a woman. While she reached enlightenment, she heard the cries of humans suffering and her compassion grew strong and she decided to stay to help those in need returning to be a bodhisattva of compassion. Some Vietnamese people fleeing their country during and after the Vietnam War immigrated to the US in small boats across vast expanses of the sea. Many of those people recounted seeing Kuan Yin on their journey, protecting them from storms and keeping them safe until they arrived in the US. Call on Kuan Yin when you feel the need for compassionate protection.

Prayer to Kuan Yin:

> *Her mind is virtue, perfected.*
> *Her body is wisdom, perfected.*
> *Her face is bathed in Holy Light.*
> *She is Compassion itself.*
> *Her orchid heart delights in Mercy.*
> *No matter what evils we face,*
> *No matter what beasts or demons,*
> *No matter what ill-fortune or disease,*
> *No matter even if we face death,*
> *Kuan Yin destroys them all,*
> *With her Compassionate glance,*
> *With her perfected soul.*
> *She is infinitely blessed.*
> *Let us bow to her in prayer.*[3]

---

[3] http://www.templeofthegoddess.org/PrayerRequests/kuanyinpoet.htm

QUESTIONS FOR REFLECTION – COMPASSION

How does compassion with love show up in your life?	
Is anything difficult for you about compassion? Forgiveness?	
Think about suffering with another. What would that look like for you?	
Compassion is empathy in action. Think about where you could be more empathic in your life.	

COMPASSIONATE FORGIVENESS RITUAL FOR FALL EQUINOX

To prepare, choose an event or a relationship in your life that would benefit from compassionate forgiveness. Choose one that is not too intense. It is better to begin this practice with events or relationships that only require a little more attention. Once you have done this a few times, you can try it with more difficult relationships or events. Prepare your altar with items that bring you comfort, along with your regular items. If you use cakes and ale, prepare edible items that you loved as a child. Have two candles on your altar, one for yourself (any color you choose) and a blue one for Kuan Yin. Use an incense that you particularly appreciate. You may want to record the meditation.

Wear comfortable clothes and wash your hands.

Ground.

Light the candles and incense.

Cast the circle as a sphere, a comfortable and cozy place for your ritual.

Call the quarters, asking at each direction for their compassionate nature – Air: soft breezes, gentle butterflies, etc. Fire: soft candle flame in a dark room, a fire on a cold night, etc. Water: a warm bath, a soothing caress, etc. Earth: a soft bed of leaves to sit upon, the stillness of the forest at midnight, etc.

FALL EQUINOX OR MABON – COMPASSION

Take a deep breath and stand in front of your altar. Be prepared for meditation.

Say: *May the Peace of Kuan Yin be upon this household.*
May the Light of Kuan Yin be in my soul.
May the Wisdom of Kuan Yin be in my mind.
May the Virtue and Purity of Kuan Yin be among the members of my household.
May the Health and Well-being of Kuan Yin be manifest throughout my body,
And radiate through the garments I wear.
May the Grace of Kuan Yin be in my worship.
May the Talents and Genius of Kuan Yin be manifest through my senses.
May the Peace of Kuan Yin be upon me!

Prepare for meditation.

Close your eyes and take a deep breath. Relax your face. Relax your throat. Relax your arms. Relax your torso. Relax your legs. Relax your feet. Let everything you had to do today be done and bring yourself into present time.

Visualize a place for yourself where you feel peaceful and safe. Look around. What does it look like? Are you inside or outside? Which colors are present? What do you hear? If it is not already present, visualize an altar – and on the altar, watch as a thousand-petalled lotus appears. You hear faint music all around you. As you look at the lotus, pick one of its petals. This represents the event or relationship you wish to give compassionate forgiveness to.

Hold it in your hands and remember the event or relationship. Let the feelings which arise surface and flow into the petal.

When you are completed, look again at the altar and see Kuan Yin sitting in the lotus. She is holding a jar of pure water and holds a willow branch … she smiles the most loving smile you have ever seen. Hold up your petal to her as an offering.

She touches you gently with the willow branch, and compassion flows easily to your heart … your heart is filling with compassion … next she offers you the jar of pure water … place your petal in the water … as you look, the petal is gently transformed into a golden light … it disappears into the pure water.

The compassion in your heart grows stronger … you feel more compassion for others and give yourself all the compassion you need … you feel light and free in your heart and your entire body … Kuan Yin smiles and reminds you she is always available when you need compassion … she says, "Good human, here at the Fall Equinox as we are, and thankful for what the Earth provides, we look with compassion on all Earth's creatures." Bow in gratitude to Kuan Yin … she gives you a small pouch as a gift … take a look in the pouch … what has she given you?

Fill your body with gratitude for Kuan Yin's gift and your ability to feel compassion. Kuan Yin now leaves and disappears into the lotus. The lotus melts into the altar. The altar now disappears and you can feel your body. Take a deep breath and open your eyes.

Bow to Kuan Yin at your physical altar and express your gratitude for her visit.

Enjoy your cakes and ale, giving the first to Kuan Yin. Perhaps play some soft, soothing music.

When you are done, bade farewell to Kuan Yin in your own words.

As you release the directions, appreciate them.

Open the circle and offer a benediction: *Blessings have been given; Blessings have been received. May the compassion of Kuan Yin remain in my heart. So Mote It Be.*

Touch the floor or ground.

Samhain or Halloween – Honor

Samhain, the Pagan New Year, is the consummate liminal time on the Wheel of the Year. We experience the 'thinning of the veil' between the worlds of the physical and non-physical. The physical world is the one we experience with our bodies. The non-physical world we experience with our psychic perceptions, our imaginations, and our third eye or the 6th chakra. It is in the non-physical where we journey in pathworkings and meditations. There we can encounter deities, the Fae, elemental beings, ancestors (family or chosen), and other beings without bodies – and some may even perceive the potential future.

Honor has two meanings. One meaning is "to regard with great respect." We honor our ancestors (family or chosen) at Samhain to remember their role in our lives and respect the life they lived and how they contributed to ours and others. We can also regard with great respect the entirety of the non-physical, which is crucial to our own well-being. The non-physical is as real as the physical. It is where we exist between lifetimes and prepare for our next lives. The non-physical also holds our many lifetimes of memories, and many beings only exist in the non-physical.

Another meaning of honor is "to fulfill (an obligation) or keep (an agreement)." Perhaps you have an obligation from a loved one to take on a task they requested. My mother, on her deathbed, asked me to find her brother and let him know she had passed. I did not know her brother and they had not spoken for a very long time. I did finally find him after many years of searching on and off, which was so gratifying. I felt honorable in the deepest part of myself to have fulfilled one of her dying wishes. Maybe your loved one asked for an agreement to be kept, such as a particular wish for burial or distribution of property. Honoring our loved ones and their wishes at death helps us become stronger in our self-esteem. When we 'walk our talk', our integrity grows. We honor our words and display honor in our deeds.

Our awareness of death is heightened at Samhain as it is the typical theme of this Sabbat for Pagans. Very early in my Pagan life, a couple of friends and I decided to do a Samhain ritual in an old house that was part of a university campus we all attended. We chose a room that was empty and rarely used, and set up our circle. I recall feeling so clearly that the house was full of spirits, that the non-physical was present with us all the time and that we only needed to shift our consciousness to be aware of them. They respected our circle and I did not feel fear. Rather, I was amazed that I could 'see' them and had never noticed them in this building previously. Perhaps you have had such experiences or have felt the presence of your loved one after they leave the body. Samhain is the time where it seems easier to communicate with those that we have lost and hear what they have to tell us. As a clairvoyant, I am very clear that the non-physical is not somewhere else, but right near us always. I've often thought the non-physical is just another dimension from this one or a different vibration to ours, but co-located in terms of space. However, biocentrism tells us that space and time are properties of our minds and have no reality outside of our minds. Time is the experience we have of change.

Space is not validated by Einstein's theory of relativity, and quantum physics tells us that what appears as empty space is full of particles and fields. Everything is entangled with everything else, even galaxies apart. This validates that the non-physical and the physical are intertwined.

Let's take a moment here to discuss death. The United States culture, where I live, appears to glorify violence that leads to death, but we are not comfortable with actual death. We no longer take care of our loved ones' bodies after they die, as in previous generations. We now give their bodies over to professionals so that we do not have deal with actual death. As Pagans, we see death as part of the cycle of life. All around us we see nature living, growing, maturing, dying, and transforming back into living all the time. The seasons show us the same pattern; and thus, at Samhain, we encounter death as part of our Wheel of the Year. For humans, death is the end of a living human body, for without the spirit or being of a person, the body cannot survive. Now we are faced with what we believe about the afterlife. Pagan ideas about the afterlife would likely be as varied as non-Pagans. Many Pagans would find comfort in the image of the Summerland, a place of rest and renewal before reincarnating. Some may find the work of Robert Monroe fascinating for afterlife information.[1] Some may see afterlife stories and images from a variety of indigenous cultures more satisfying. What afterlife story do you believe? What will you tell your children?

In biocentrism, it is argued that there is *no death* because consciousness cannot be nonexistent. Even to be able to perceive nonexistence would require consciousness. This perspective brings a new meaning to the concept of death.

---

1 Monroe, Robert. Journeys Out of the Body. Harmony, 1992.

SAMHAIN OR HALLOWEEN – HONOR

Death is just a moment in time when our consciousness leaves the body and we continue as non-physical beings. The idea that death is a final result and ends with self-oblivion, or that there is nothing after death, is misguided according to biocentrism. Many psychics who can regularly see non-physical beings that used to be physical would make the same argument, including myself. Can we as Pagans reform the concept of death in our communities? Can we reframe it to show that moving into the non-physical is a movement in consciousness? Even the Death card in the tarot rarely shows physical death; rather, a significant change in the querent's life or the ending of something that leads to a new situation. *The Light Seer's Tarot* tells us that the Death card indicates that "the energy of transmutation and rebirth signals a metamorphosis that will allow you to expand your consciousness and move closer to your divine essence." It is helpful to expand our understanding of death and remove the societal fears and misunderstandings.

For those of us remaining after a person has transitioned to the non-physical, we feel the grief of the loss of the experience of them in the body. While grief is an emotion we must work through, we can find some comfort as Pagans in understanding that death is a transition to the non-physical and does not mean that we lose contact – just physical contact. We often say "what is remembered, lives." This concept is graphically illustrated in the wonderful movie *Coco*, which specifically argues that remembering keeps the non-physical intact. While that concept may not be actually how reality works, it illustrates that the relationships we have do not end with the transition to the non-physical and, in fact, we can demonstrate honor in our lives by acknowledging and celebrating those relationships through all transitions.

Thus, at Samhain, many of us remember the dead, and also welcome the newly born – affirming the cycle of life. Take some time at Samhain to think of your own death. What do you hope for yourself? Who do you want to be present at your dying, if anyone? Would you want music played? Would you want to chant or would you say a meaningful poem or liturgical passage? If you believe, as many Pagans do, in reincarnation, then what do you want in your next life? While these questions sound very personal, talking about them with your loved ones is important. They need to know what you want at your dying moments. In circles and family gatherings, tell stories of any deaths you have experienced. Ask yourselves, what is a good death?

Honoring the answers to these questions is imperative. You and your loved ones may not always agree, but what *you* want is what is to be honored. It is their role to honor agreements and fulfill obligations. Perhaps this is the time to put together all important documents, create an advanced healthcare directive, a will and after-death arrangements. This is how you can honor those left behind once you leave the body.

For those of us left after a loved one has passed, I believe we need more robust grieving rituals/practices in our Pagan communities. Many religions have specific practices after a death, and I've often thought we still need markers of grief for those of us who may need to be out in the world while in grief. I recall that after my mother died, I could barely fathom that the world kept turning and life was continuing as 'normal' when my world had been so utterly changed. I offer that we could adopt such practices as black and orange wreaths or ribbons on our homes to designate that we are in grief. In our US culture, black is still thought of as the appropriate color of clothes for a funeral. As Pagans, we know that black is the color for rich possibilities, which we would see in a grieving process as knowing that our loved one is looking at all the possibilities for another life. We could wear black with a green or orange armband – green for our Pagan sensibilities, denoting the cycle of life, death and rebirth – or orange as a color of Samhain. We could wear such armbands for 13 days after a death or multiples of 13 or for a year and a day. After a year and day, we may need to reflect on our grief process. If sadness and grief are still preventing us from living fully, we might seek grief counseling to help us handle our grief. What other practices would you adopt for grieving?

Honoring each other is a form of love. Honor is given without thought of response. We see the goodness in people when we honor them. We see the kindness in people when we honor them. We see the courage in people when we honor them. We see the love in people when we honor them. We not only honor people, we honor this planet that is our home, that graciously accepts our dead and our tears. We honor life itself and the cycle of life renewing itself, time and time again. In our loving eyes, we see the multitude of ways to honor our world, our ancestors and ourselves.

Samhain asks us to visit the liminal place between life and death, to move easily in that space and gain wisdom from that movement. The greatest wisdom at this time is found contemplating an honorable life well-lived.

This is a quote from an elementary school in North Carolina: "When you act with honor, you do the right thing regardless of what others are doing. You keep your promises, without anyone reminding or nagging you. You honor your elders by speaking respectfully to them. You honor yourself by being your best and practicing your virtues every day. When you act with honor, you set a good example, not to be admired, but just because it is the right thing to do."[2]

Prayer to Hekate:

Hekate, she who is the World Soul, who gives us the keys the universe, we praise you at Samhain. You who know the way between the worlds, light your torch so that we may find our way to honor our ancestors of blood, choice or magic. You who helped Persephone return to her mother. You who helped Demeter embrace her grief; help us find honor in ourselves, in our lives, by your excellent example. Hekate, Chthonia of the Earth/Underworld, help us honor death as part of the great circle of life. Beneficent goddess, we honor you this day and ask for your blessings.

---

[2] http://hhes.ccs.k12.nc.us/files/2012/06/honor.pdf

QUESTIONS FOR REFLECTION – HONOR

How will you express honor in your life?	
Think about being an honorable person. What does that mean to you?	
Discuss after-death preparations with your loved ones. Have you made your arrangements?	
Create an ancestor altar in your home to honor them. Who would you include?	
Write your own obituary.	

HONOR YOUR ANCESTORS AT SAMHAIN

To prepare, create or clean up your ancestor altar. To create an ancestor altar, place pictures of your *honored* ancestors on an altar, separate from your regular altar. If you have a white cloth, use that for the altar cloth. Prepare foods which your ancestors enjoyed or find objects they owned or used. If you use cakes and ale, prepare food and drink to enjoy with your ancestors. Hekate will be used in this ritual, but you can decide which deity you want to call.

Dress in dark ritual clothes and wash your hands.

Ground, deeply and strongly.

Cast your circle and call the quarters as you typically do at Samhain.

Invoke Hekate. Use your own words or use this invocation:

Hekate, Chthonia.
She who moves between the realms,
She who helps the dead to peaceful repose.
Mighty Goddess of the Crossroads,
Where the living and the dead meet.
Your black hounds guide us to your mysteries,
Your keys guide us on the path of knowing.
Mighty Hekate, Chthonia and Soteria, our World Soul,
Call my ancestors forth to join in this circle that I may speak with them,
And hear their wisdom.
Blessed Be.

Feel the power of Hekate in your circle. See if you can feel your ancestors with you. Take up their picture and speak what is in your heart to them. Honor their life and their place in your life. Spend as much time as you want. Offer your food and drink to them and eat and drink with them. Perhaps play music they liked while you eat.

Offer gratitude to your ancestors. Think about how your family or chosen family will talk about you when you are an ancestor. Will they say that you lived an honorable life? How do you want to be remembered?

When you feel complete, thank Hekate and bade her farewell.

Release the quarters and open your circle.

Offer a benediction: *Blessings have been given; Blessings have been received. May the honor of Hekate remain in my heart. So Mote It Be.*

Touch the floor or ground.

Afterthoughts

We have now journeyed together around the Wheel of the Year, contemplating the virtues in *The Charge of the Goddess* and how they can improve our lives and relationships. We have learned what a "good person" might look like in our Pagan traditions.

As a Pagan Community Minister, it is my wish that you either use these virtues as additions to your practices or that you put your own virtues on the Wheel of the Year. I fervently hope this small book begins a conversation among Pagan folk about what it means to be a good person in our traditions, which could be a bridge to inter-faith encounters. The Abrahamic faiths could all answer this question. Buddhists could answer this question. Philosophers could answer this question. There is no reason that Pagans could not answer this question as well. Remember that the ancient world produced Aristotle, who was a participant in this topic. If a cursory search is made about the ideas of a good person in the ancient world, we see many different ideas – which is what we would expect from a Pagan world.

While most Pagans believe that we are born good, remaining a good person is a choice. Using these virtues is one way to contemplate this question and learn what being a good person means to you, and whether you will cultivate virtues in your journey around the wheel. Perhaps there are other spiritual poems or liturgies that inspire you in this process. In any case, striving for such an understanding appears to have many benefits. Physical health benefits, mental health benefits, relationship benefits and self-related benefits. *The Charge of the Goddess* asks us to embody the virtues discussed: "Let there be beauty and strength, power and compassion, honor and humility, mirth and reverence *within you*." It is my hope that this meditation on those virtues around the Pagan Wheel of the Year has been illuminating and inspiring to readers.

> "A peaceful heart is reward alone for being a good person."
>
> – Anonymous

www.ingramcontent.com/pod-product-compliance
Ingram Content Group UK Ltd.
Pitfield, Milton Keynes, MK11 3LW, UK
UKHW020943230325
456615UK00005B/127